SYLVIA'S BOOK OF

MACRAMÉ LACE.

UNIFORM WITH THIS VOLUME.

THE CHILD'S FANCY WORK AND DOLL BOOK.

THE LADY'S LACE BOOK.

ORNAMENTAL NEEDLEWORK.

London: Ward, Lock, & Co., Salisbury Square, E.C.

SYLVIA'S

BOOK OF

MACRAMÉ LACE.

CONTAINING

ILLUSTRATIONS OF MANY NEW AND ORIGINAL DESIGNS,

WITH COMPLETE INSTRUCTIONS FOR WORKING, CHOICE
OF MATERIALS, AND SUGGESTIONS FOR
THEIR ADAPTATION.

LONDON:

WARD, LOCK, AND CO., WARWICK HOUSE,

SALISBURY SQUARE, E.C.

PREFACE.

———•◦•———

THIS kind of fancy work is not exactly a novelty, except in the sense that when anything becomes so old as to be forgotten, its revival has all the effect of a first appearance. It is a beautiful and effective lace, costing little difficulty to the worker, and useful in a variety of directions. It is an exceedingly fashionable occupation, and in addition to presenting our readers with the clearest instructions yet issued upon the subject, we have also the satisfaction of offering, in the present volume, the largest number and greatest variety of designs that have hitherto been collected together.

PREFACE

This kind of fancy work is not exactly ⟨illegible⟩ ⟨illegible⟩ in the sense that when anything becomes ⟨illegible⟩ its revival has all the effect of ⟨illegible⟩ beautiful and effective lace, costing ⟨illegible⟩ and useful in a variety of directions ⟨illegible⟩ fashionable occupation, and in addition to ⟨illegible⟩ with the clearest instructions yet ⟨illegible⟩ have also the satisfaction of offering ⟨illegible⟩ largest number and greatest variety ⟨illegible⟩ been collected together.

INDEX.

		PAGE
Articles of Dress, &c.		376
,,	Cravats	376
,,	Hanging Work-Case ...	381
,,	*Illustrations of*, 379, 382,	383
,,	Side-Pocket	381
,,	,, *Illustrations of*, 368,	
		369, 373,	378
,,	Work-Bag	377
,,	,, *Illustrations of*, 372,	373
Fringes		311
,,	for Antimacassars	311
,,	,, *Illustrations of*, 294 to	297
,,	Border with Fringe	321
,,	,, *Illustration of*	304
,,	for Dresses or Furniture ...	317
,,	,, *Illustrations of*, 300,	301
,,	for Dresses	332
,,	,, *Illustration of* ...	314
,,	Fine Thread Fringe	319
,,	,, *Illustration of*...	303
,,	for Furniture	335
,,	,, *Illustrations of*, 316,	317
,,	for Parasols	326
,,	*Illustrations of*, 308, 309,	312
,,	Silk Fringe	319
,,	,, *Illustration of* ...	302
,,	for Trimming Dresses, &c....	322
,,	,, *Illustrations of*, 305 to	307
,,	for Various Purposes ...	313
,,	,, *Illustrations of*, 298,	299
Insertions		337
,,	Fine Thread...	337
,,	,, *Illustrations of*, 320,	321
,,	for Underlinen	346
		PAGE
Insertions for Underlinen, *Illustra-*		
	tion of	325
,,	for Various Purposes ...	342
,,	,, *Illustrations of*, 322 to	324
Macramé Lace, Instructions in ...		289
,,	Cushion	292
,,	Genoese Knot	306
,,	,, *Illustration of*	292
,,	Grounding	310
,,	,, *Illustration of*...	293
,,	Solomon's Knot	307
,,	,, *Illustration of*	292
,,	Materials for...	291
,,	Stitches	293
,,	,, *Illustrations of*, 290,	291
Various Household Articles		348
,,	Bag for Bathing Dress ...	370
,,	,, *Illustrations of*, 358,	359
,,	Basket for Layette	371
,,	,, *Illustrations of*, 362,	363
,,	Collar	356
,,	,, *Illustrations of*, 340,	344
,,	Towels	354
,,	,, *Illustrations of*, 332 to	335
,,	Towels	366
,,	*Illustrations of*, 348 to 353,	356
,,	Watch-Pocket...	373
,,	,, *Illustrations of*, 364,	365
,,	Window-Blind...	355
,,	,, *Illustrations of*, 338,	339
,,	Window-Drapery	348
,,	,, *Illustrations of*, 325, 328,	329
,,	Work-Bag	361
,,	,, *Illustrations of*, 340,	341

MACRAMÉ LACE.

MODE OF WORKING.

Introduction—Materials—Cushions—Various Stitches—Knotted Bar—Star or Diamond—Genoese Knot—Solomon's Knot—Grounding.

THIS fascinating kind of fancy-work dates as far back as the fifteenth century. The materials are inexpensive, and the lace lasts almost for ever. The work progresses rapidly, and can be made in many materials; none, however, so good as the cord made and sold for the purpose. The manipulation consists in tying knots of various kinds. This lace can be unhesitatingly recommended as a pleasant occupation and pastime.

Goethe, somewhere or other, in exalting music above every other art, does so on the ground that it produces its marvellous effects with so little display of means and tools; and if this test be applied to our present work, it will rank very high amid the rival styles of lacemaking and embroidery. No dazzling range of colours, no blending of different materials, not even a thimble and needle, are wanted to produce the charming effects of our Macramé work.

And first of all, why "Macramé?" Macramé is nothing but the name given by the Italians round about Genoa (the home and birthplace of the work) to a coarse material used for towels, the fringed ends of which are knotted in several of the lace stitches which we shall afterwards explain. As to the materials required, they are of the simplest. We advise our fair reader to begin with the coarse Macramé thread until she has learnt how to wield her weapons, and thoroughly mastered every

MACRAME

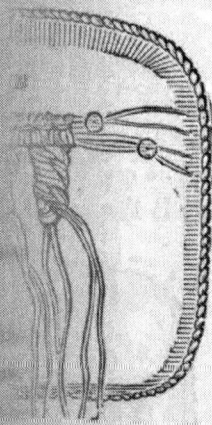

WHOLE KNOT.

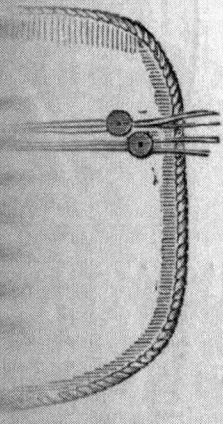

...lks made specially for
...e white linen, brown,
...or coloured linen and

stitch;' but when that is once done, she will find herself able to
work rich trimmings for black and coloured costumes both for

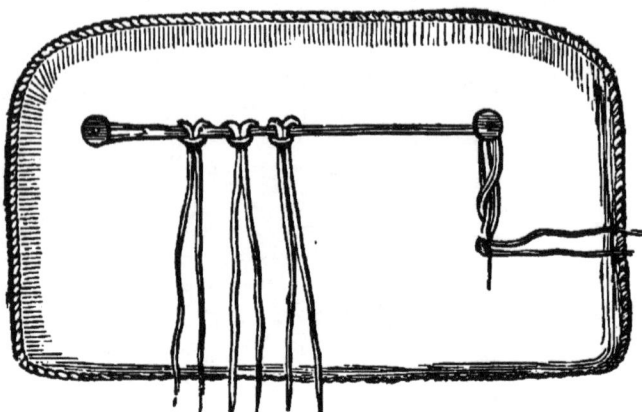

339.—MINIATURE CUSHION, WITH FOUNDATION THREAD, AND
PUTTING ON OF THE STITCHES.

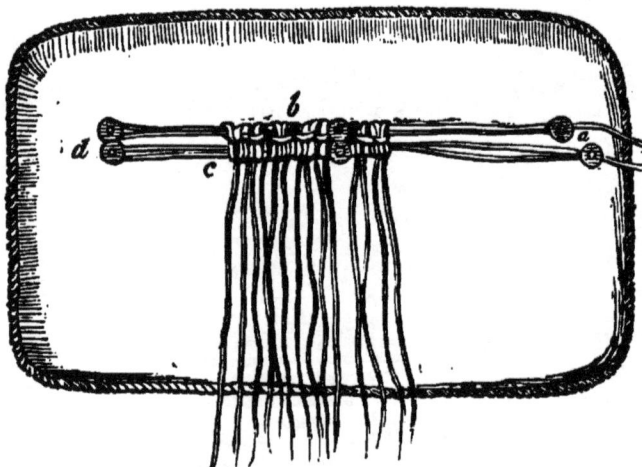

340.—FIRST ROW WITH A CORD.

home wear, garden parties, and seaside rambles—fairylike
adornments for household and underlinen—fringes, edgings, and

insertions for towels, pillows, antimacassars—covers for sofa-cushions, etc., etc. For these latter purposes she will have at

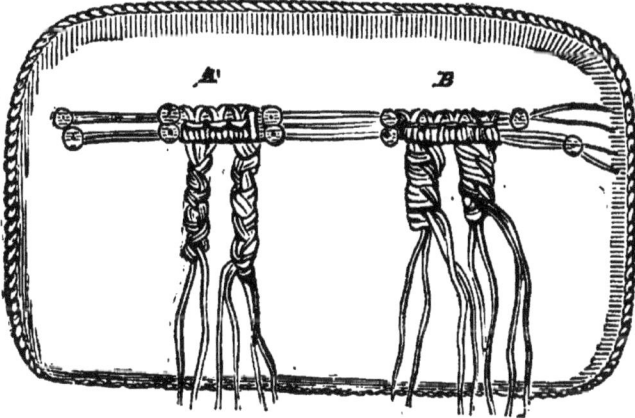

341.—KNOTTED BAR.   BUTTONHOLE KNOT.

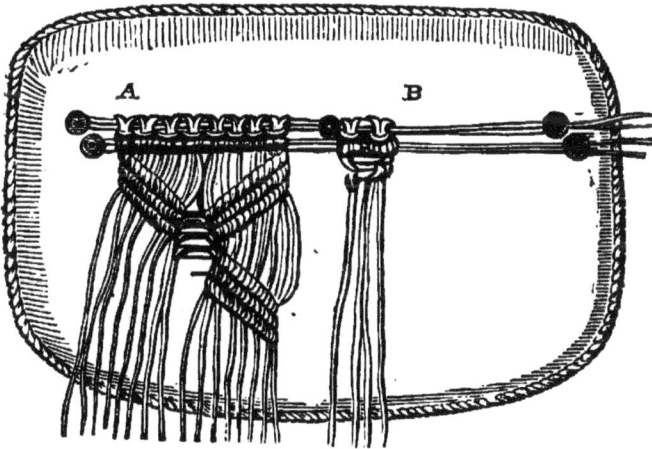

342.—DIAMOND OR STAR.

her command black, white, and coloured silks made specially for Macramé work, very fine flax thread for the white linen, brown, grey, and all shades of écru for unbleached or coloured linen and holland materials, filoselle for fancy trimmings, and so on in endless variety. But, being a beginner, she will at first try "her 'prentice hand" on the coarse Macramé thread generally preferred for trimming brackets, drawing-room tables, mantelpieces, etc.

The first thing wanted is a weighted cushion, measuring about ten inches long by seven or eight wide. The best way is to get a bag of coarse towelling of the dimensions above given, and stuff it carefully with sand and bran well mixed; the sand will give it the necessary weight, and the bran is easy to stick

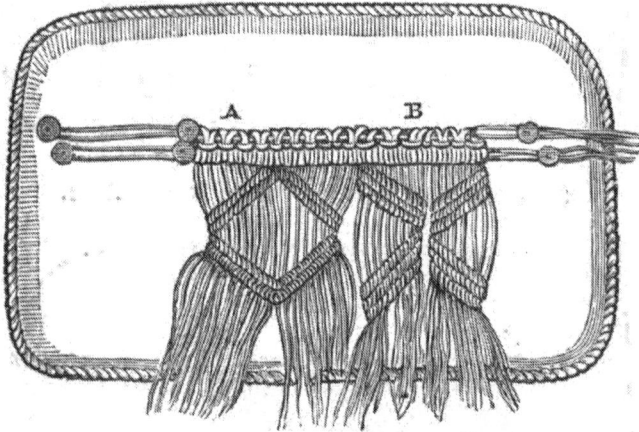

343.—GENOESE KNOT.   SOLOMON'S KNOT.

pins in. As to the cover of the cushion, we strongly recommend a fine dark cloth; some people advise a striped material, such as ticking, saying that the lines are a help in stretching the horizontal threads, but in our opinion the lines are often rather confusing than helpful, and we believe our pupil will find them wholly unnecessary, while cloth is much pleasanter than ticking to work upon.

The cushion made, and slightly rounded at the top, the learner will provide herself with a box of steel toilet-pins with glass heads, sold for the purpose, and she will take care to have them of bright colours, so as to make every process of her work gay and pretty. A piece of coarse thread, double the length of the lace required, is then folded in half, and pinned on the left side of the cushion as it faces the worker. This double thread is called the "foundation thread," and is pinned horizontally across the cushion. A number of doubled threads—say half a yard long when doubled—are cut ready and fastened on to the foundation thread, as shown in Illustration 339.

Look at the illustration, and having pinned the foundation

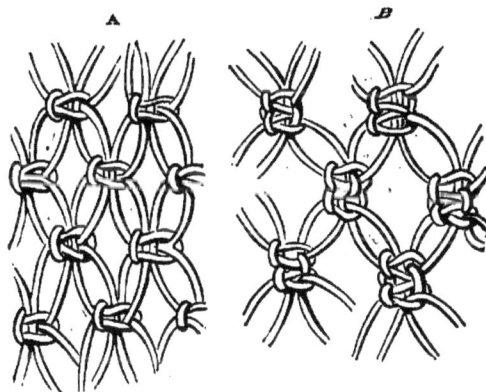

344.—DESIGNS FOR GROUNDING, OR OPEN KNOTTING.

thread as directed, take up one of the double lengths, and pass the doubled centre downwards under the foundation thread, so that the two ends are lying across the far side of the cushion; then bring these two ends through the loop you passed under the foundation thread, and draw up the stitch. The first row of every pattern is worked in this way by putting on as many threads as are wanted.

The next thing to be learnt is the Macramé knot, which enters into every pattern, and is used in marking what is called the cord—a pretty, close pattern, generally following close upon the first row of the work.

Macramé Lace.

The cord and Macramé knot illustrate each other, and are
better learnt together. We suppose that the foundation thread
is stretched upon the cushion, and the first row worked according
to Illustration 339. Now consult Illustration 340.

You will notice that a second double foundation thread has
been pinned on close to the stitches of the first row, and it is
along this second thread that the cord is worked. The foun-

345.—Detail of 350.

346.—Detail of 350.

347.—Detail of 350.   348.—Detail of 351.   349.—Detail of 352.

dation thread is pinned at first only on the left side of the
cushion, and must be held raised a little from the cushion in the
right hand. Now take up in your left hand the first single
vertical thread *, pass it over and then under the foundation
thread and through the loop made by itself; draw up tight, and
repeat from *. Proceed in the same manner with every thread in
succession. Our illustration gives a useful hint to the learner by

showing the use of pins to hold the stitches well in place and close together; and we may add that care should be taken not to split the thread, but to stick the pins between two threads; also to be careful to take the threads in their proper order. Having worked the cord, there only needs a word as to the Macramé knot. It is worked exactly as above described, the

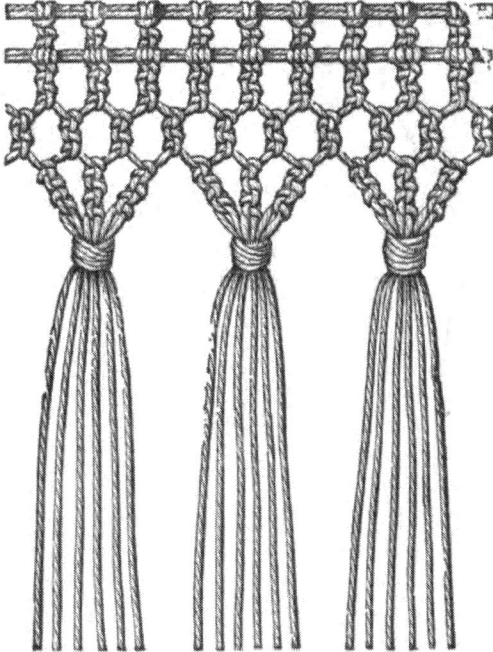

350.—Fringe for Antimacassars, &c.

stitch being formed twice with the same vertical thread, as it is the second half of the stitch which holds the first in place.

We come now to the Knotted Bar. This is a useful stitch, and enters largely into all patterns. We again suppose the cushion before you, with its cord neatly worked along the second foundation row. Now consult Illustration 341.

You see that in the examples given four threads are used in

éach bar. Beginning, then, with Fig. A, work with the two
left-hand threads a single or half Macramé knot over the next
two threads, and then work the same knot with those threads
over the first two. Repeat this alternately, and you will have
accomplished the double Macramé knot shown in Fig. A. It is
called double because it is worked with two threads, not be-

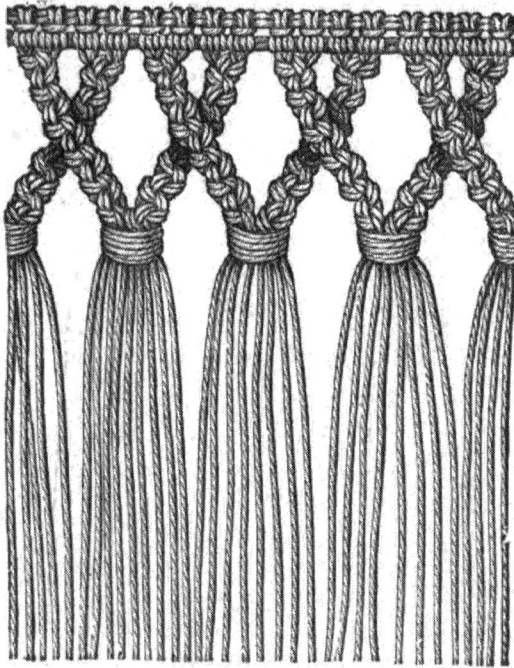

351.—Fringe for Antimacassars, &c.

cause it is worked twice with the same threads. We give no
further illustrations of this bar. Our fair pupil has already
divined how it may be worked with single instead of double
thread, with three over three, with half or complete Macramé
knots, and so on. When she has exercised her skill in all these
varieties she should turn to Fig. B, and work the buttonhole

knot. Again four threads are required; take three threads in
the left hand, in the right hand take up the fourth thread, pass
it over and then under the three threads, and draw it up, this
time not too tightly. The same remarks apply to this useful
knot as to the one represented in the preceding figure; varia-

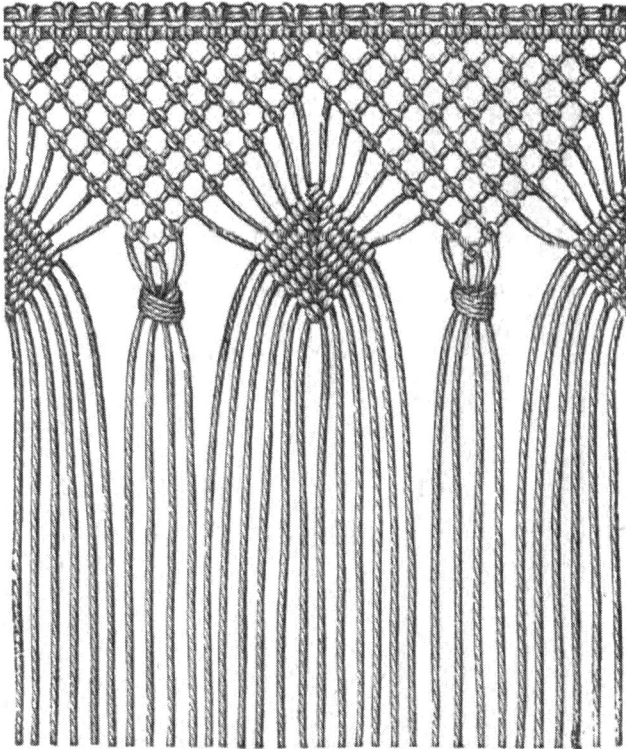

352.—FRINGE FOR ANTIMACASSARS, &c.

tions of it will be easily recognised in patterns of Macramé
work, and will be copied without difficulty.

The next thing to be mastered is the Diamond or Star Pattern. We say " or" advisedly, for the one is but a variation of
the other. On looking at the best styles of Macramé lace, it

will be almost always found that this figure is worked imme-
diately beneath the cord described in Illustration 340. We give,
therefore, in the following diagram the usual heading of the
preceding illustrations. Now consult Illustration 342.

Sixteen single vertical threads must be set aside for this

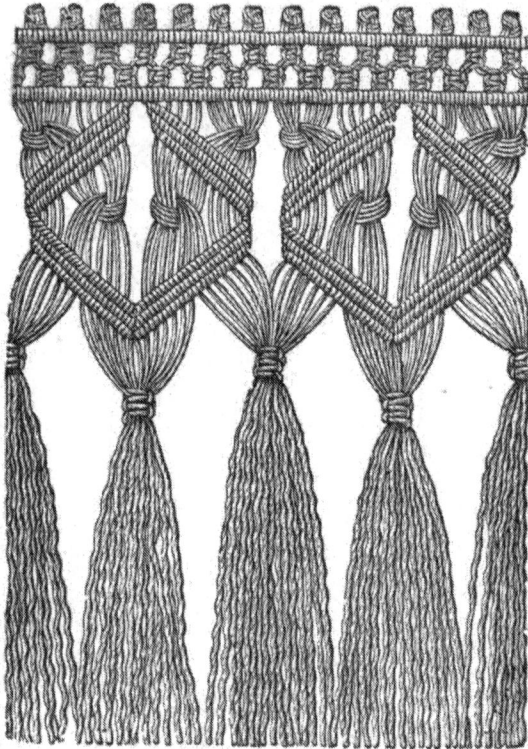

353.—FRINGE.

pattern; and for the present the eight right-hand threads had
better be twisted round a pin, and fastened on to the cushion,
out of the way. The pattern is now begun with the eight left-
hand threads, as follows:—Take the eighth, or right hand, thread
in your left hand, and hold it diagonally over the other seven

298

threads, letting it slope downwards at the angle shown in the diagram. This thread is technically known as the "leader:" it is better to keep the term "foundation" threads for the horizontal ones. Now take the seventh thread in your right hand, and work over the leader a complete Macramé knot, keeping the

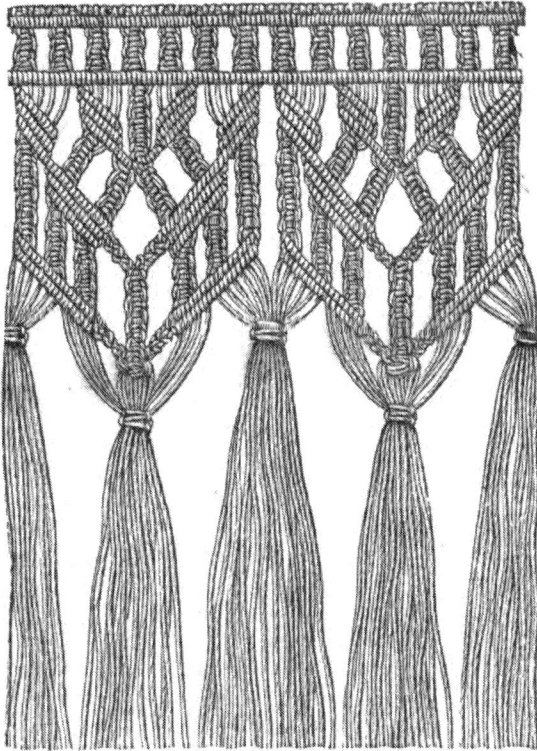

354.—FRINGE.

leader carefully in position. Repeat the Macramé knot with every thread in succession down to the first, and pin the leader to the cushion. In some patterns only one leader is used, but, as our diagram represents a double diamond, you will now take the seventh or right-hand thread as a second leader; place it

299

close to the first, and work over it with every thread in succession a Macramé knot, as before, of course, taking in the thread which formed the leader in the last row. Now unpin your

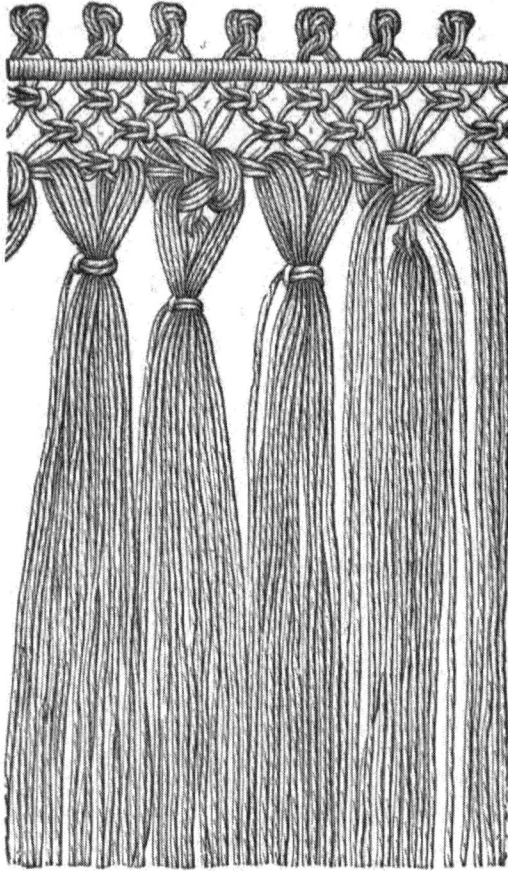

355.—MACRAMÉ FRINGE.

second group of eight threads. Take the first for the leader, and hold it diagonally across the other seven; take the second thread, and work a Macramé knot over the leader, do the same with every thread in succession, and pin down the leader as before. Then take the second thread for your leader, and work over it the second row of Macramé knots. By this time you will see that the upper half of your diamond is achieved. Use

356.—MACRAMÉ FRINGE.

pins freely in this part of the work, that your diamond may be true and firm. Now take the first left-hand thread as leader, slant it downward to the centre of the diamond over the other seven threads, and work your row of Macramé knots; then use the second thread as leader, working over it the second row. To finish the diamond, take the outer right-hand thread of the second group, and slant it down to the centre, work over it the row of Macramé knots; then take what is now the outer right-

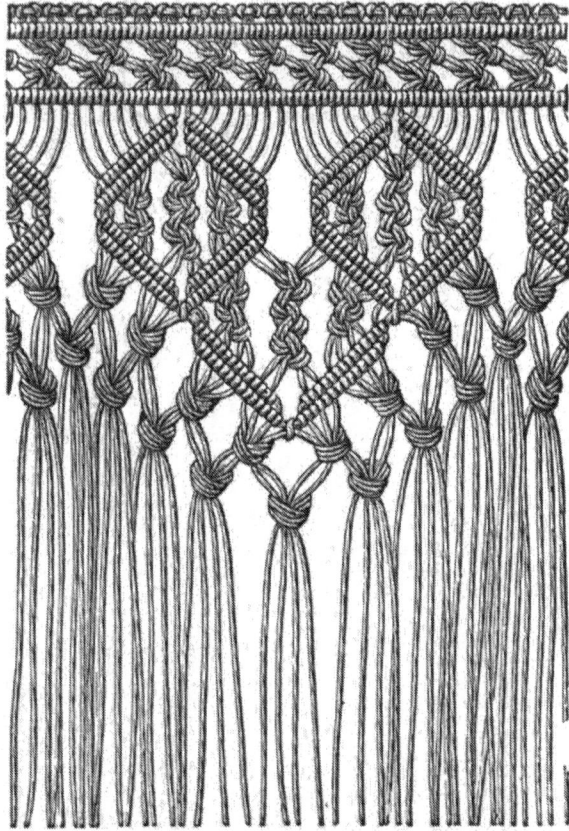

357.—MACRAMÉ FRINGE.

hand thread as leader, and work the second row. Lastly, tie the two centre threads together in a Macramé knot. By this time, we hope, the diamond is a complete success, and that our fair reader is already devising many an original combination to vary the one just worked out as an example. As to the star, it is nothing but a diamond reversed—that is, it is begun with the first, or left hand, thread as a leader, and when half completed it is joined in the centre by tying two threads in a Macramé

358.—MACRAMÉ FRINGE.

knot, as we directed in describing the diamond pattern. The three diagonal lines in Fig. B will often be claimed as old acquaintances in Macramé lace, although they may form no part of either star or diamond, and we hope that in whatever com-

Now turn to Illustration 343, where you will recognise the half-completed star, with its centre Genoese knot. It is now supposed that the star has been joined together in the centre, and we begin our directions from that point. Take the four centre threads; we will number them from left to right, as 1, 2, 3, 4. Hold 1 tightly in the left hand, and with the right hand pass 4 over 3 and 2, under 1, over 1, under 2 and 3, and draw up

361.—MACRAMÉ FRINGE.

closely, but not too tightly; repeat eight times, so that you have a flat bar hanging vertically from the work. Now take a medium-sized bone or wooden knitting-pin, and lay it horizontally across this bar, take up all the four threads, pass them over the knitting-pin, above the knot which joined the star, thread them through the opening, bring them out again below the knitting-pin, and tie them tightly; then remove the knitting-pin, and finish the star. The diagram shows in Fig. B a knot called sometimes a Josephine and sometimes a Solomon's knot. It is often used to form a heading, but when four Solomon's knots are tied in a diamond shape they make a pretty centre to the larger diamond, shown in Illustration 342. For the Solomon's knot proceed as follows:—Take the centre four threads of a pattern, or four threads of a straight row, and

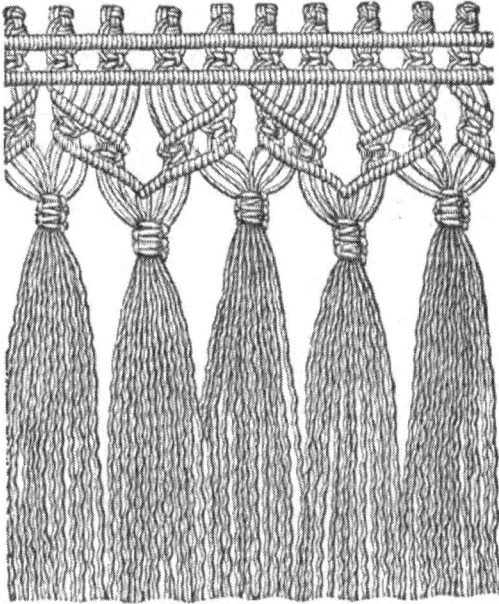

362.—MACRAMÉ FRINGE.

call them, as before, 1, 2, 3, 4. Hold 2 and 3 straight down the cushion; bring 1 across them, so that it forms a loop, then take 4 in your right hand, bring it downwards over the end of 1 (which is lying horizontally across 2 and 3), pass it under 2 and 3, and bring it upward through the loop between 1 and 2. Then take the threads one in each hand, and draw them up close. This is one-third of the knot. Then, still keeping 2 and 3 hanging straight down, take up 4, pass it across them

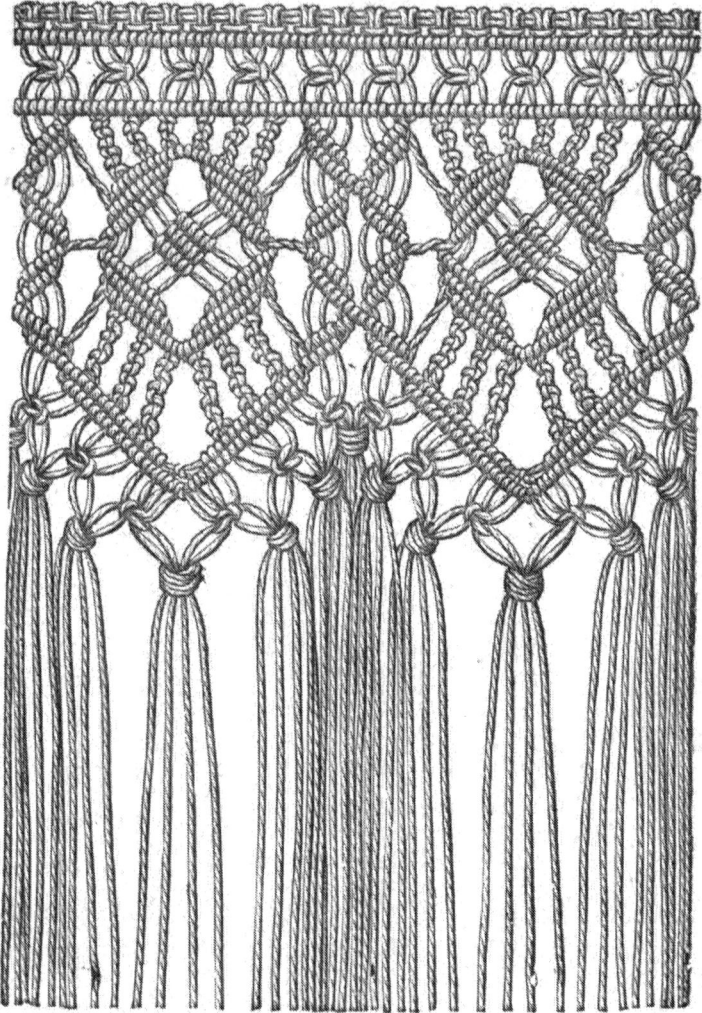

363.—FRINGE FOR PARASOLS.

from right to left, so as to make a loop, take 1 and pass it downward over the end of 4 which is lying horizontally across 3 and 2,

308

pass it under **2 and** 3, and bring it up through the loop formed

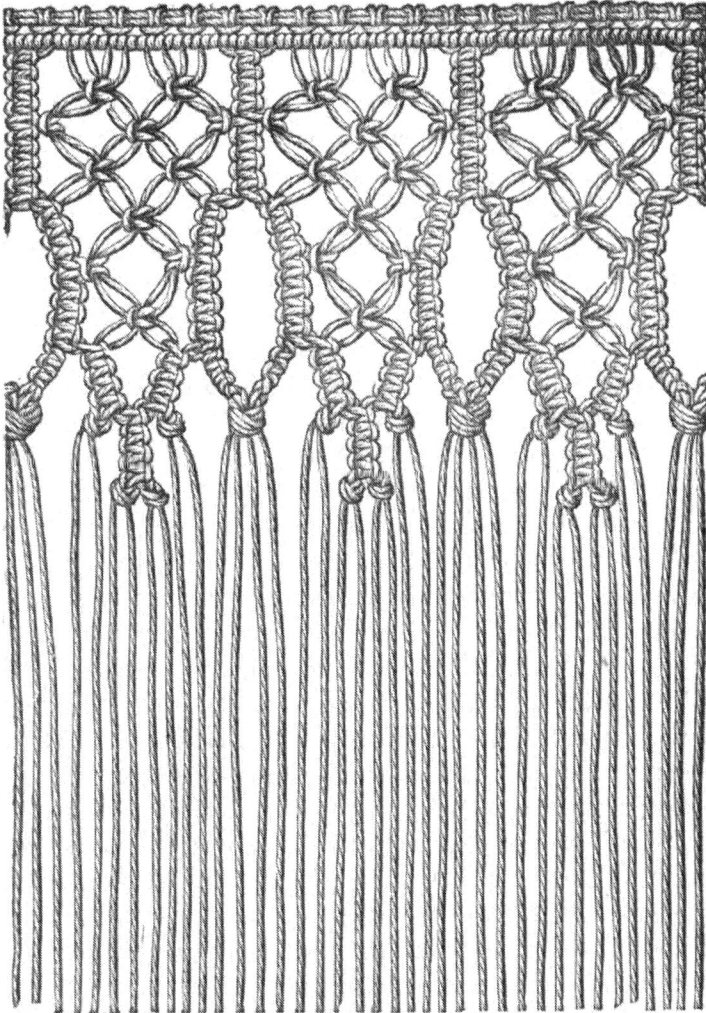

364.—FRINGE FOR PARASOLS.

by 4, between 3 and 4. Take the two ends, and draw them up
close. This is the second part of the knot. The third part is

nothing but a repetition of the first, and it must be remembered that the complete Solomon's knot consists of these three parts.

In every stitch for which we have given directions so far the thread has been always closely drawn up, and the lines sharply horizontal or diagonal. Our next illustration shall give examples of what is sometimes called open knotting, and it will be found very useful to form a kind of network or filling up between the more sharply defined parts of a pattern. It may spring from almost any part of the work, and therefore it is represented in the diagram without the usual indication of the cushion, or any heading. Consult Illustration 344, and begin with Fig. A, as the simpler pattern. The stitch is worked with four threads, from left to right. Keep the two centre threads straight down, and do not let them get crossed. Pass the first thread over the second and third, and under the fourth; pass the fourth under the third and second, and through the loop over the first, draw up close, but not very tight; then, working from right to left, pass the fourth thread over the third and second, and under the first, then the first under the second and third, and through the loop over the fourth, and draw up close, but not very tight. This forms the knot. The next knot will not be made with the same four threads, but the last two threads will be knotted to the first two threads of the following knot, and so on. By this time, with the aid of your pins, which are always useful in keeping the work in place, and by consulting the intervals left in the diagram for the circles and curves, the pattern will soon be reproduced upon the cushion, As to Fig. B, it is worked with four threads in exactly the same way, only the knot is made twice instead of once, as will be clearly seen on examining the diagram. In treating of knotted bars, with the help of our third diagram, we contented ourselves with explaining the two there represented; but a very simple and effective bar is sometimes made by merely tying ordinary knots with two or four threads, working alternately from right to left and left to right.

FRINGES.

For Antimacassars—Dresses—Mantles—Parasols—Cravats—Furniture, &c.

Nos. 345 to 352. Fringes for Antimacassars, &c. The materials selected for the fringes may be either thread, silk, wool, or fine cord. No. 350. Take a double thread of the length required for the fringe, fasten to the left and right side of the cushion, letting the loose end hang free. At intervals, along this double thread, a piece of thread folded in half is knotted as shown in Illustration 345. Each knotted thread is fastened to the cushion with a pin, and then the first row is worked with the double thread hanging towards the front of the cushion. Make a knot like a double buttonhole stitch, as shown in No. 347, holding quite straight and firm the thread round which the knot is made. 2nd row: Fasten a second horizontal line of double thread to the cushion, and, beginning at the left hand, make a double buttonhole stitch over it, as shown in Illustration 346. 3rd row: Like the first, only that 2 knots, instead of 1, are made. 4th row: Like the last, except that the knots are made between the 2nd of 1 double thread, and the 1st of the following one. 5th row: Like the last, but knotting 3 instead of 2 knots. In the 6th row 3 instead of 2 threads are knotted together; and the ends are cut off in regular lengths. No. 351. This fringe is begun like the preceding one, but in the 2nd row 6 double knots are made, as shown in Illustration 348. The rows of knots are then fastened together, as shown in illustration. No. 352 is begun in the same way, but the first row is knotted like the 2nd row of No. 350. 2nd row: Lay the 2nd end of the thread to be knotted over the 1st end, and make with the latter 2 buttonhole stitch knots. This kind of knot is made in the 9 following rows, and a glance at the illustration will show which ends are to be knotted together. The netted pattern having been framed, the four strands of thread at the point of the vandyke are knotted together, and the close pattern between the vandykes is knotted

365.—PARASOL.

as follows:—Take the 7th of the 12 threads, lay it across the first 6 threads, and work from right to left, making 2 button-hole stitch knots with each of the 6 threads ; then place the 6th thread over the 5 last of the 12, and proceed in the same manner from left to right. (See Illustration 349.)   Complete the close pattern in the same way, using the 8th, 5th, 9th, and 4th threads, and so on, as the 7th and 6th were used.

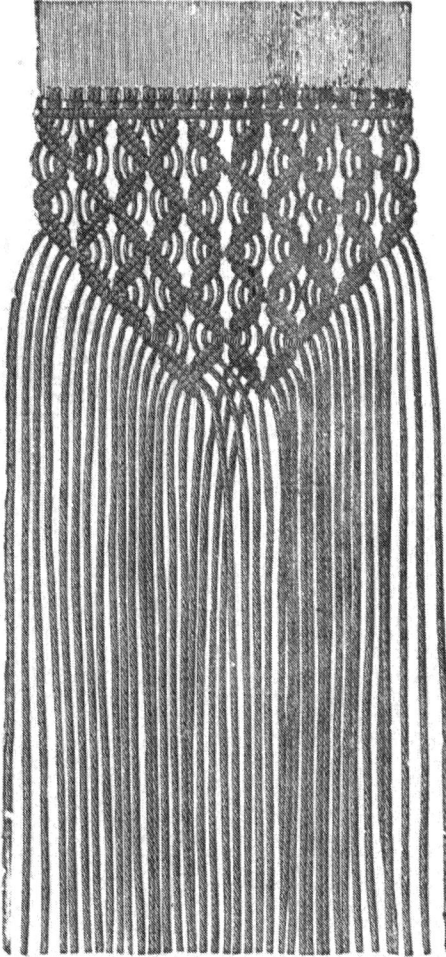

366.—ORNAMENTAL FRINGE FOR ENDS OF CRAVATS.

No. 353. Fringe. (Macramé Work.) Materials: White or écru-coloured thread. For illustration, fold in half 14 strands, each measuring 24 inches long, knot just where they are folded in half, every 2 strands together (of course there are 4 single strands in the 2 doubled ones), knotting the 3rd and 4th over

367.—Fringe for Dresses, &c. 368.—Fringe for Dresses, &c.

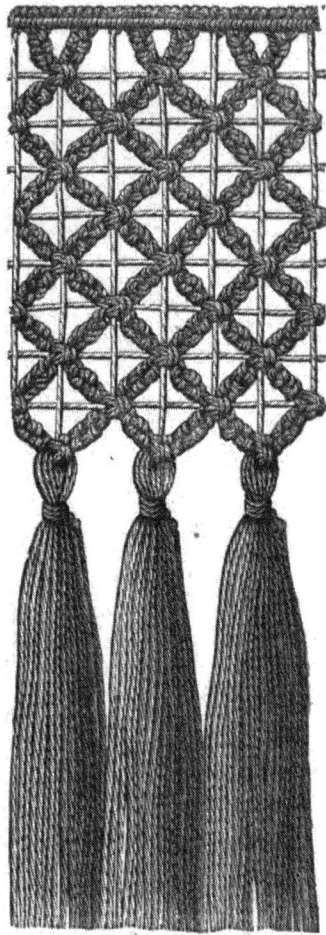

the 1st and 2nd, and then the 1st and 2nd over the 3rd and 4th, 14 strands make one pattern. Having then begun as many patterns as you intend to knot, fasten the strands with a pin on

to a weighted cushion, and place a double horizontal thread
close under the knots. 1st row: Work from left to right as
follows :—2 buttonhole loops with every strand over the horizontal threads. 2nd row: 2 double knots with every 4 strands.
3rd row: The same, but in reversed position. 4th row: Like
the 1st row. 5th row: The intervals between the rows must be
copied from the illustration, and the strands are numbered as
they occur in each row. * Make a loose knot with the 5th to
the 8th strand, round the 1st to the 4th. † Place the 14th
strand aslant over the 13th to the 1st, and work 2 buttonhole
knots with each strand in order (13th to 1st) over the 14th ;
repeat twice from †. Then knot the same pattern, but reversed
(see illustration), and repeat from *. 6th row: Like the preceding, but in the order shown in the illustration. 7th row:
Take the centre 14 strands of a pattern, and work a double knot
with the 1st and 14th strands over the 12 between, then do the
same with the last 7 of one pattern and the 1st of the next, and
cut the ends even.

No. 354. Fringe. Tie on to a double foundation thread a
number of folded strands, each 24 inches long and divisible by
14. 1st row : 2 buttonhole loops, with each strand in succession over a double foundation thread. 2nd row with 4 strands :
2 buttonhole loops, with the 4th over the 3rd and 2nd together,
2 buttonhole loops, with the 1st over the 2nd and 3rd, repeat.
3rd row: Like the 1st row. 4th row : * With 28 strands, 1
knotted row like the 2nd row, with the centre 4 of the 28
strands, but instead of the 4 double buttonhole loops 7 of
them, † ; 1 leaf as follows : place the 1st strand aslant over the
2nd to the 6th, and work 2 buttonhole loops with each over the
1st, repeat twice from †, then a similar leaf, with the 7th to the
12th strand, with the 17th to the 22nd, and the 23rd to the
25th : these last must be knotted in reversed position. The last
knotted row of the two centre leaves are continued to the centre,
for which purpose two buttonhole loops are added with each of

the two first of the centre 4 strands over the foundation thread. The continuation of the pattern may be clearly seen from the illustration. The centre 16 strands of each pattern and the

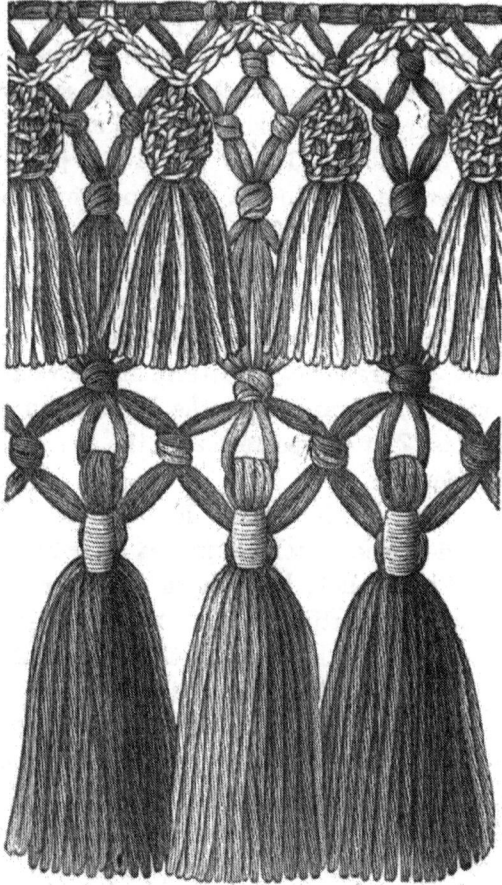

369.—FRINGE FOR FURNITURE.

last 6 and first 6 of each pattern are then knotted together as in the fringe described in No. 353.

No. 355. Fringe. (Macramé Work.) Made with fine thread.

Furniture Fringe.

Take a number of strands of thread, about 12 inches long, and
fold them in half, two at a time, then knot a loop with the 3rd
and 4th strands over the 1st and 2nd, and then with the 1st

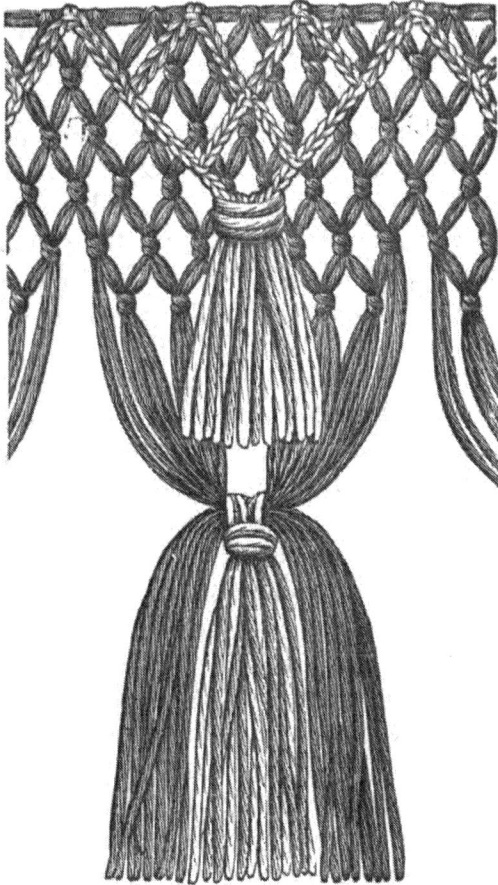

370.—FRINGE FOR FURNITURE.

and 2nd over the 3rd and 4th. Fasten each of the knots to the
weighted cushion with a pin, and knot the 1st row as follows:—
Place a double foundation thread horizontally across the ends

and close under the knots. Work from left to right, and knot with each strand 6 buttonhole knots over the foundation thread. Twelve strands make one pattern. 2nd row: 1 double knot with every four strands. 3rd row: 2 double knots with the 3rd to the 6th and with the 7th to the 10th, leaving the 1st and 2nd and 11th and 12th unnoticed. 4th row: 1 double knot with the 5th to the 8th, leaving unnoticed the 1st to the 4th and the 9th to the 12th strands; then with every 12 strands work 1 double knot, using the four centre strands as a foundation thread. To each knot add 4 new strands, folded in half, and tie them round for a tassel, as shown in the illustration. Then add 4 new strands to those left unnoticed in the 4th row, and tie them in the same way for a tassel. When the work is finished, cut the strands even.

No. 356. Fringe for Dresses or Furniture. (Macramé Work.) Material: Orient wool. Cut a number of lengths about 12 inches long, and folding them in the centre two at a time, make a loop with the 3rd and 4th ends over the 1st and 2nd; and then with the 1st and 2nd over the 3rd and 4th. Fasten each knot so made on to the weighted cushion with a pin and then knot the first row as follows;—Lay a double foundation thread of wool horizontally across the ends and close under the row of knots. Work from left to right 2 buttonhole knots with each end over the double foundation thread. 2nd row: Take the 4th thread and work 4 buttonhole knots over the 1st, 2nd, and 3rd threads, repeat. 3rd row: Leave unnoticed the threads of the first bar of buttonhole knots, * take the thread of the next bar and knot with it 4 buttonhole loops over the previously used 3 foundation threads, repeat from *. 4th row: Like the 1st row. 5th row: * 4 buttonhole loops with the 1st end over the 2nd and 3rd; then 4 buttonhole loops with the 6th over the 4th and 5th, repeat from *. 6th row: 1 double knot with the 1st and 6th strands over the 2nd to the 5th. Then cut the fringe even.

No. 357. Fringe. (Macramé Work.) Along a double foundation

thread knot strands of écru thread or purse silk, folded in half, and measuring 28 inches. Illustration 357 shows how this is done. Work from right to left. 1st row: Place a double thread across the strands and work 2 buttonhole knots over it with each strand in succession. 2nd row: 1 chain knot with the first 4 strands; this is done by knotting in buttonhole loop with the first 2 over the second 2, and then with the second 2 over the first 2. 3rd row: Like the preceding, but in reversed positions, taking the 2 last ends of one set of 4 to work with the first 2 of the next set of 4. 4th row: Like the 1st to the 5th row. * Leave a space as the illustration shows, divide into 16 strands, place the 8th strand slantwise over the first 7, and use it as a foundation thread; work 2 buttonhole stitches in succession over it from the 7th to the 1st, and do the same with the 10th to the 16th over the 9th; repeat from *. 6th row: A close row of knots like the preceding. 7th row: With the centre 4 of the 16 strands 3 chain knots as in the 2nd row, then with the 4 strands on each side 1½ chain knots; repeat from *. 8th and 9th rows: Like the 5th and 6th rows, but in reversed position, and in the 9th row knot the centre 2 of the 16 strands so as to form a little square. 10th row: With the centre 12 of the next 32 strands, 1 pattern as described in the 7th row. 11th and 12th rows: With centre 16 of 32 strands. 1 pattern like that of the 8th and 9th rows. 13th row: Knot every 4 strands. 14th row: Like the 13th, but in reversed position. The strands are then cut level.

358. Fringe. (Macramé Work.) Along a double foundation thread, knot a number of strands of thread, folded in half and measuring about 32 inches long. The number must be divisible by 6. 1st row: With a double thread laid across the strands, 2 buttonhole stitches with each strand over the horizontal thread. 2nd row: 12 strands are required for one pattern, * 1 double knot, with the 3rd to the 10th strand, using the centre 4 as a foundation, and the outer ones to form the knots, 1 double knot

319

with the 11th and 12th, and 1st and 2nd of next pattern, repeat from *. 3rd row: * Place the first of the 12 strands slantwise over the 2nd to the 6th strands, and knot with each of the latter 2 buttonhole knots over the slanting strand, place the 12th strand aslant over the 11th to the 7th, and knot as above, repeat from *. 4th and 5th rows: Like the 2nd and 3rd, but with the

371.—MACRAMÉ INSERTION.

pattern in reversed position. 6th row: Like the 2nd. 7th row: Like the 1st. 8th and 9th rows: Like the 2nd and 3rd. 10th row: 1 double knot, with centre 4 strands of each pattern, leaving the other strands untouched. 11th row (see illustrations for distances): * Place the 6th strand aslant over the 5th to the 1st, and work with each of the latter 2 buttonhole stitches over the 6th, place the 7th over the 8th to the 12th strand, and

320

work over it as above, repeat from *. 12th row : * 1 tatted knot with the 2nd over the 1st, and with the 11th over the 12th. 1 double knot as before, with centre 8 strands. 13th row: Like the 3rd. 14th and 15th rows : Like the 11th and 12th, but without the tatted knots. 16th row (see illustrations for distances) : 1 double knot, with each 12 strands, repeat, then

372.—MACRAMÉ INSERTION.

thread 8 strands 4 inches long through the centre of each loop, tie them round to form a tassel, and cut the ends even.

No. 359. Border for Antimacassars. (Cross Stitch and Macramé Work.) This border, which is intended for any cover which has a straight edge, is worked in cross stitch, on yellow Russian lawn, with 2 shades of claret filoselle, and is then sewn on to a slip of claret plush or velvet. Every cross stitch takes in 4 threads of the lawn each way. Below the embroidery the lawn is unravelled, and every 16 threads are tied round with light and dark red silk alternately. Then follow in reversed position 4 rows of double knots. The 16 threads required for each double knot are then tied round again with red silk, and 4 more rows of double knots are worked as before. The tassels are then tied round, as shown in illustration, and the fringe is cut even.

No. 360. Fringe. (Macramé Work.) Materials: Silk, wool,

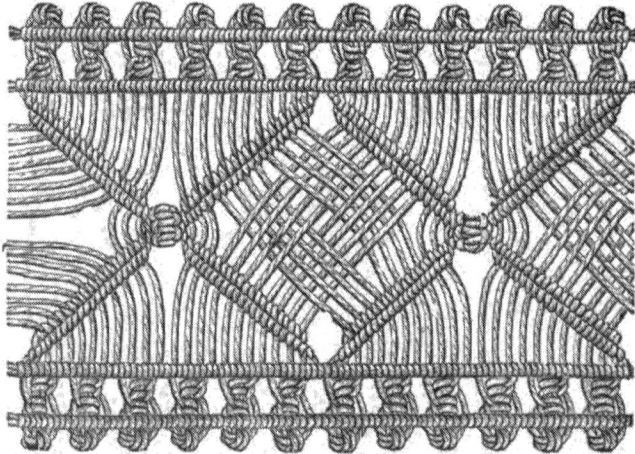

373.—Macramé Insertion.

or thread. Along a double foundation thread of the required length knot a number of strands folded in half, and work from left to right. With 2 strands, 1 tatted knot with the right strand over the left. For the next row in reversed position 1 chain knot—that is, 1 buttonhole loop with the 1st strand over the 2nd, and then with the 2nd over the 1st—then change the ends, working the knot just described with the 2nd of the 1st double strand and the 1st of the strand following; then place a new strand over the knotted strands and tie one tatted knot over it with each strand in succession, then divide into patterns

24 strands each, and continue as shown in the illustration, working the bars in the chain stitch as above described. The principal figure in each pattern is worked with Josephine knots. For every figure of the close cluster of knots which surround the Josephine knots 3 strands are required. * Use 1 strand as a foundation, over which tie a buttonhole knot with the 2nd strand, and then a similar knot with the 3rd over the 2nd; repeat twice from *, but before beginning these knots tie a double knot round the strands of the chain stitch. The close

374.—INSERTION (Macramé).

border which edges the vandyke of every pattern is tied like the knotted cluster above described; but the original foundation strand of 2 threads is strengthened after the point of the vandyke by the ends which have been left unnoticed as the pattern narrowed. The ends of the vandyke are then knotted together and cut even.

Nos. 361 and 362. Fringes. (Macramé Work.) No. 361. Along a double foundation thread knot a number of strands, 16 inches long and folded in half. 1st row: Place a double thread horizontally across the strands, and work over it 2 buttonhole loops with each strand. 2nd row : 3 buttonhole loops, with the 4th strand over the 1st, 2nd, and 3rd of every 4. 3rd row : 3 buttonhole loops, with the 4th strand over the first 3 of the next 4 strands. 4th row like the 1st. 5th row : Every pattern requires 24 strands. * With the 3rd to the 6th, and the 15th to the 18th, inclusive, 1 double knot over the 8 strands between ; then taking together the 7th and 8th, and the 13th and 14th, 1

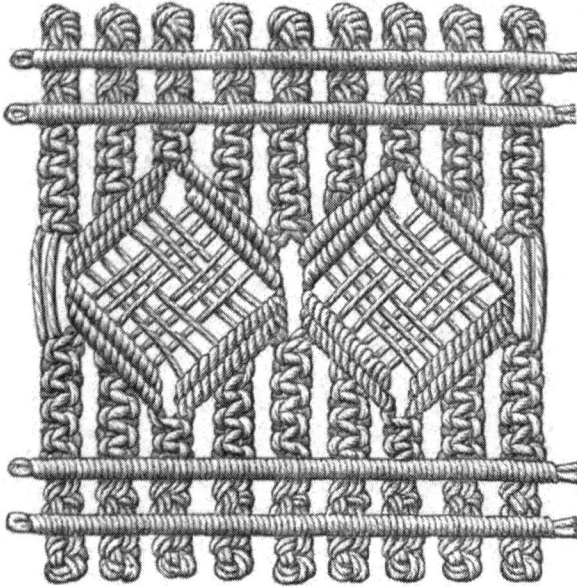

375.—Insertion (Macramé Work).

double knot over the 4 strands between ; then with the 9th and 12th strands, 1 double knot over the 2 strands between ; then 3 double knots with the 21st to the 24th strands ; repeat from *. 6th row : * Twice place the 1st strand aslant over the 2nd to the 8th, and work over it 2 buttonhole loops with each ; then twice pl⸺ ⸺e 20th strand aslant over the 19th to the 13th, and work ⸺ttonhole loops with each ; repeat from *. 7th row : ⸺th and 8th strands together, and the 13th and 14th of the next pattern, and work 1 double knot over the 4 strands between ; then take the 5th and 6th, and 15th and 16th, together, and work 1 double knot over the 8 strands between ; then with the 19th and 20th of this pattern, and the 1st and 2nd of the next, 1 double knot over the 4 strands between ; then with the

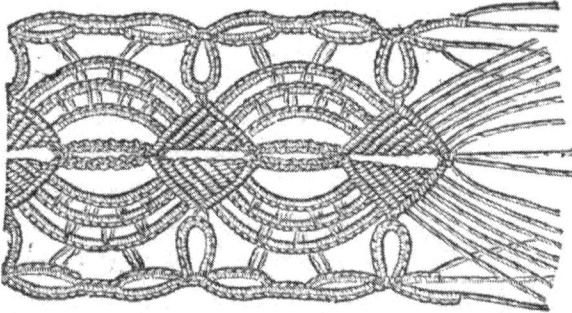

376.—INSERTION FOR UNDERLINEN.

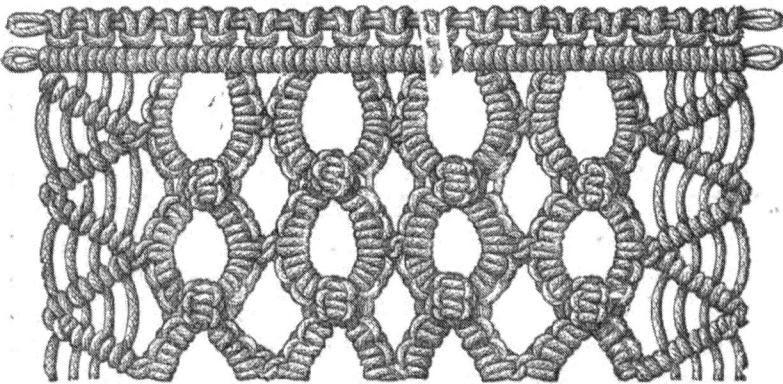

377.—DETAIL OF WINDOW-DRAPERY.

17th and 18th of this pattern, and the 3rd and 4th of the next pattern, 1 double knot over the 8 strands between ; repeat from *. Cut the ends even, and crimp them.—No. 362. The number of strands must be divisible by 8, and measure about 16 inches long. They are then folded in half, and every 2 are knotted

together in a buttonhole loop. This row of knots is then pinned
on to a weighted cushion, and the work begun. 1st row:
Place a double foundation thread across the strands, and, working from left to right, work 2 buttonhole loops with each over
the foundation thread. 2nd row: 1 double knot with every 4
strands. 3rd row: Like the 1st row. 4th row: Every pattern
requires 16 strands; the intervals must be copied from the
illustration, and the strands are numbered in the order in which
they are found when mentioned. * Place the 1st strand aslant
over the 2nd to the 8th, and work with the latter 2 buttonhole
loops in succession over the 1st; place the 16th aslant over the
15th to the 9th, and work with the latter 2 buttonhole loops in
succession over the 16th; repeat from *. 5th row: Like the 2nd
row. 6th row: Like the 4th row; but at the end of every
pattern work 2 buttonhole loops, with the 8th over the 9th
strand. 10th row: Turn back the first and last 4 strands of the
fringe on to the wrong side; fasten, and cut off the ends. * $2\frac{1}{2}$
double knots with the 5th and 12th of the next 16 strands over
the 6th to the 11th, take in the latter and use it as a foundation;
$2\frac{1}{2}$ double knots with the 13th strand of this and the 4th of the
next pattern over the 6 strands between; repeat from *. Cut
the ends even, and crimp them.

363 and 364. Fringes for Parasols, &c. These fringes may
be knotted with wool, thread, or silk. No. 363 requires a
foundation thread with strands 14 inches long, folded in half,
and fastened on at regular intervals. The 1st row is begun
from the left, two buttonhole loops being knotted with each end
over the doubled horizontal thread. 2nd row: 1 double knot
with the first 4 strands of thread. 3rd row: Like the first.
4th row: 20 strands are required for each pattern. * Take the
1st strand for a foundation thread, and, working from left to
right, make 2 buttonhole knots with each of the 2nd, 3rd, and
4th strands; then take the 8th strand as a foundation, and
working from right to left make 2 buttonhole loops with the 7th,

6th, and 5th strands respectively; then with the 9th and 10th and the 19th and 24th strands respectively make 3 double, followed by one single buttonhole loop; with the 11th and 12th and the 17th and 18th strand 2 double and 1 single buttonhole loop, with the 13th and 14th and the 15th and 16th strands 1 double and 1 single buttonhole loop; repeat from *. 5th row: * Cross the 14th and 15th strands and work from right to left, making with the 13th, 12th, 11th, 10th, and 9th ends in succession 2 buttonhole loops over the 15th strand; then from left to right make with the 16th, 17th, 18th, 19th, and 20th strands 2 double buttonhole loops over the 14th strand; then work with the 1st to the 8th strand in the same way as in the 4th row, consulting the illustration, taking in the 15th strand where the buttonhole loops end after the 1st buttonhole loop has been made with the 7th strand over the 8th; then, going back, take in the strands of thread, and then knot the 2 buttonhole loops with this 8th strand; repeat from *. At each repetition the 14th strand must be taken in with the 2nd strand of the next pattern. 6th row: * Take the 4th strand as a foundation and make 2 buttonhole loops with the 5th, 6th, 7th, and 8th strands respectively, then use the 5th end as a foundation, and make the loops with the 3rd, 2nd, and 1st strands; work in the same way with the 9th to the 20th strand as in the last row, *not* crossing the 14th and 15th strands, but always using as a foundation the strand nearest to the end where the knotting begins; repeat from *. 7th row: Like the last. The centre 2 of the 8 strands are not crossed, but knotted in the same way as the last 12 strands of this pattern; then follow 3 inserted rows as follows, which are knotted with the centre 6 of the last 12 of each pattern. In the 1st of these 3 rows the 3rd strand, in the 2nd the 2nd, and in the 3rd the 1st strand must be used as a foundation thread, and then making 2 buttonhole loops with the 4th, 5th, and 6th strands respectively; then repeat once the 4th to the 7th row, but in the reverse order, winding in the 1st row

the 7th strand round the 15th, and the 2nd round the 14th of
the previous pattern.   In the last of these 4 rows make 3 double

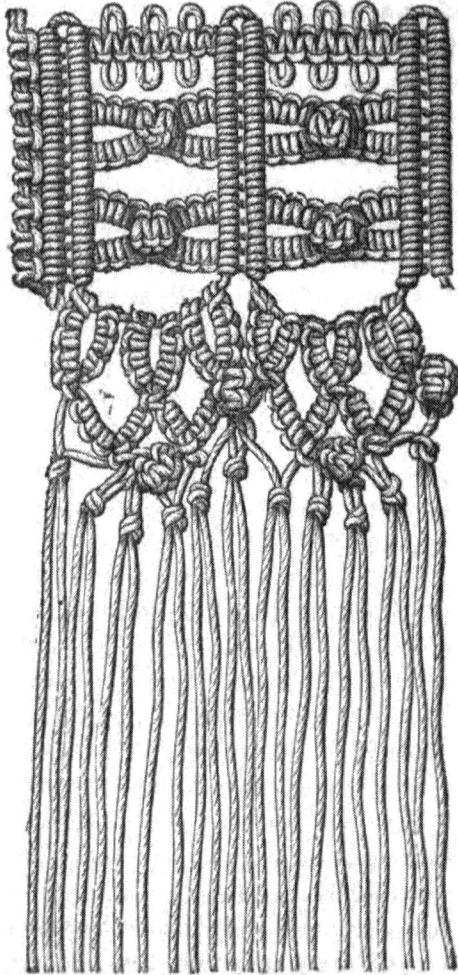

378.—DETAIL OF WINDOW-DRAPERY.

buttonhole loops with every 2 of the last 12 strands of each
pattern.   12th row: * The 1st strand of the next pattern but
one serves as foundation thread for the next pattern, making

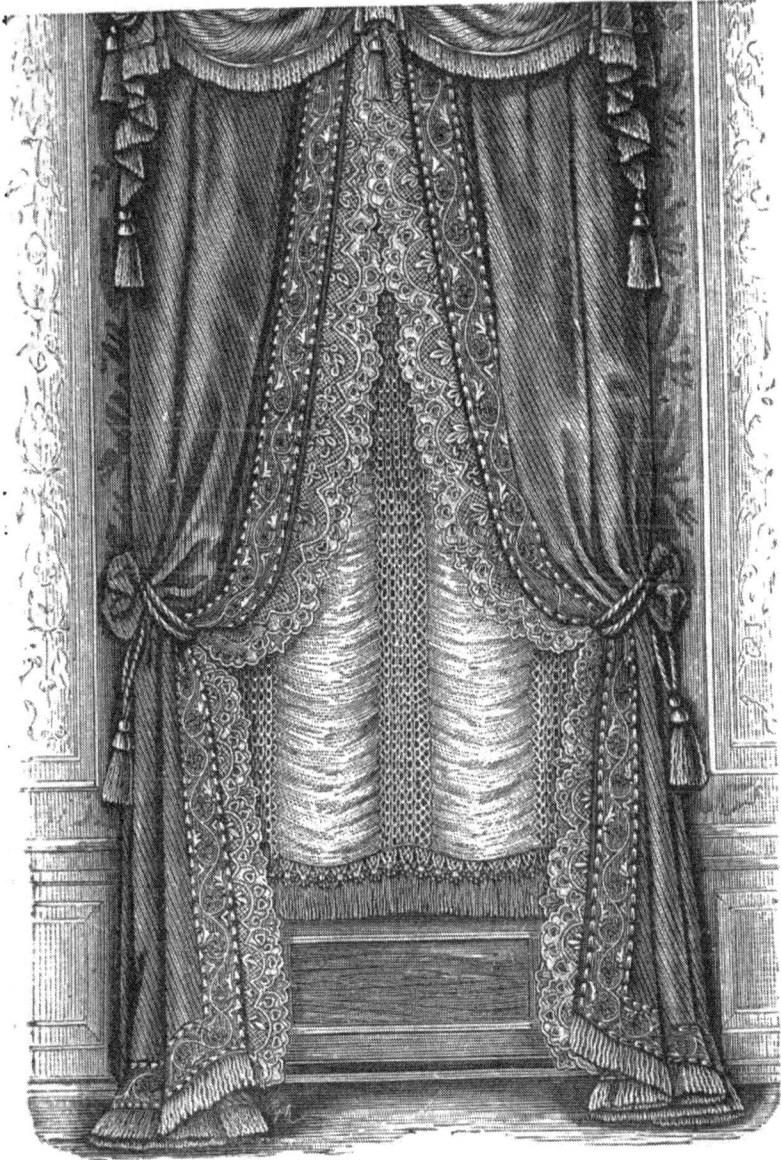

379.—WINDOW-DRAPERY.

over it 2 buttonhole loops with the 20th, 19th, 18th, 17th, and 16th strands respectively, with the 15th strand 4 buttonhole loops over the same; then take the 8th strand as a foundation, and make over it 2 buttonhole loops with the 9th, 10th, 11th, 12th, and 13th strands respectively, and with the 1st strand of the following pattern, which has been previously used as a foundation thread. 4 loops are then knotted with the 14th strand, the other strands are left unnoticed; repeat from *. 13th row: Like the last. The 7th strand is used as the foundation for the first 6 strands, and the 2nd strand of the next pattern but one is used as the foundation for the last 6 strands of the next pattern. Instead of the 4 buttonhole loops worked with the 14th and 15th strands, only 2 must be knotted, and with the first end of the next pattern which formed the foundation thread of the last row work 2 buttonhole loops. 14th row: Like the 2nd. Then knot together the 4 next ends as shown in the illustration, and cut the ends even. 364. The first 2 rows are knotted in the same way as in the last pattern. 2nd row: * 4 double knots with the first 4 strands, close to the knots in the last row. Twice (with the next 4 strands) 1 double knot; repeat from *. 3rd row: Leave the next 3 ends unnoticed, * 1 tatted knot with the following strand over the next 2 strands, 1 double knot with the next 4 strands, 1 tatted knot with the next strand but 2 over the first 2 strands, leave the next 2 strands unnoticed; repeat from *. 4th row: Like the 2nd row. 5th row: Leave unnoticed the first 2 ends, * 3 double knots with the following 4 strands, close to those of the previous row, 1 double knot with the next 4 strands, 3 double knots with the next 4 strands close to those of the previous row; repeat from *. 6th row: Leave the first 5 strands unnoticed, * 1 tatted knot with the next strand over the next 2 strands, 1 tatted knot with the next strand but one over the 8 previous ends, leave 6 ends unnoticed; repeat from *. 7th row: Like the 5th, but 4 double knots must be made instead of 3. 8th row: Leave 2 strands unnoticed, * 3 tatted knots with the next strand over the next strand. Twice (with the next 4 strands) 4 double knots, 3 tatted knots with the next strand but one over the previous strand; repeat from *. 9th row: * Knot the first 4 strands close to the knots of the previous row, knot the next 2 strands close to the other knots, 4 double knots with the next 2 strands, then knot every 2 strands together; repeat from *; cut the ends even.

No. 365. Parasol. Parasol of écru batiste, lined with white lutestring, and edged with the knotted fringe for which we gave directions in the preceding paragraph. Cane stick with silver chain and handle, in which is set a rock crystal.

No. 366. Ornamental Fringe for Ends of Cravats. (Knotted Work.) For this pretty trimming the material required is purse silk of the same colour as the cravat. Knot together 20 ends of about 14 inches in length, folded in half and placed within the hem of the cravat. These ends are fastened with a few stitches and knotted across with a double foundation thread, which is also fastened to the cravat, and passed horizontally across the 20 ends. 1st row: Take the threads in succession, and make with each two loops like a buttonhole stitch over the foundation thread. Fasten the latter carefully at the end of the row. 2nd row: 8 strands of thread form a pattern. Take the first strand for a foundation thread, and make with the next 3 strands 2 buttonhole loops each, over the foundation thread from left to right; then, working from right to left, make 2 buttonhole loops with the 7th, 6th, and 5th strands over the 8th, used as a foundation thread. 3rd row: Like the second. 4th round: Take the 4th and 5th strand of a pattern; use the latter as a foundation thread, and make 2 buttonhole loops across it, leaving the other strands unnoticed. Repeat 5 times the 2nd to the 4th row, reversing the position of the design. In the third repetition only the centre 32 strands, in the 4th only the centre 24, and in the 5th only the centre 16 ends, leaving the others unnoticed. After the knotted work is over the ends are cut even.

Nos. 367 and 368. Fringes for Dresses, Paletots, &c. (Ma-

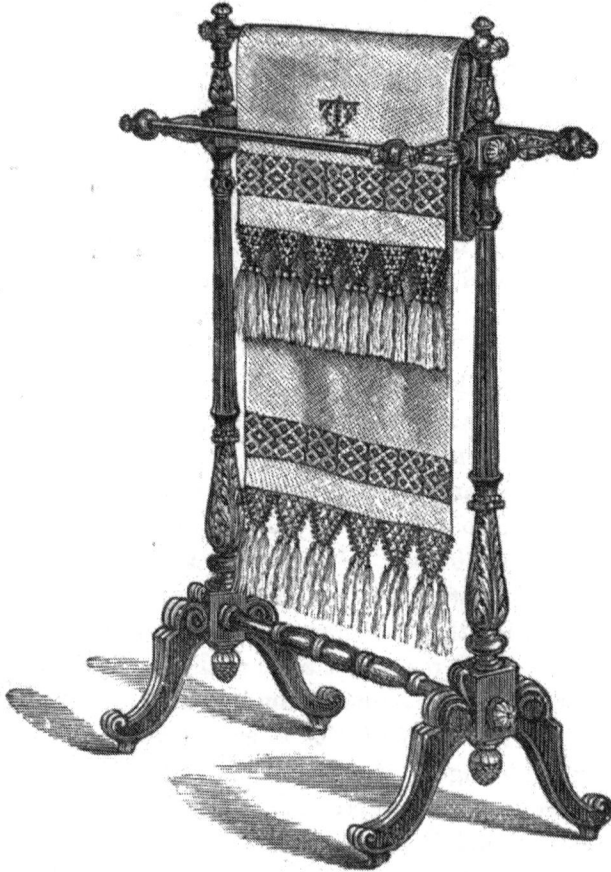

380.—Towel-Horse and Towel.

cramé Work.) These patterns may be knotted with black or coloured purse silk and fine gold thread. No. 367. Along a double foundation thread of black silk knot a sufficient number of silk strands 16 inches long and folded in half. 1st row:

Towel Fringe.

Place a double thread horizontally across the strands and work
over it 2 buttonhole knots with each strand in succession.   2nd

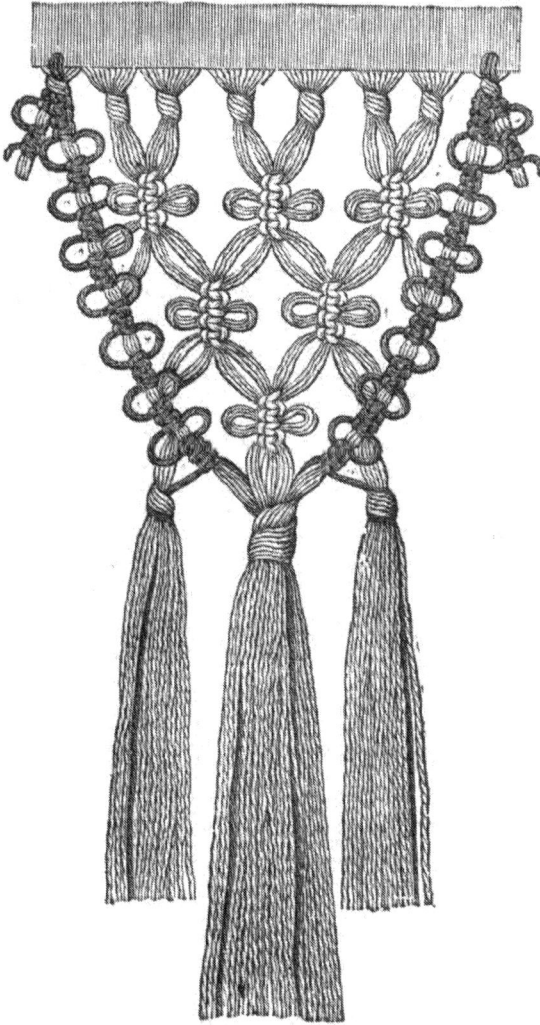

381.—DETAIL OF 380.

row: Each pattern requires 12 strands, * 3 times alternately place the 1st strand across the 2nd to the 6th (diagonally) and work over it 2 buttonhole knots with each in succession; then using the 12th strand as a leader, work a similar pattern in reversed position with the 7th to the 12th strands. Then thread through the knots of the 1st row a gold cord folded in half and measuring 4 inches long, so that it falls between the diagonal lines of each pattern. 3rd row: * 1 double knot over the gold cord with the 5th and 6th and 7th and 8th of the 12 strands; then consult the illustration and repeat the 2nd and 3rd rows, letting

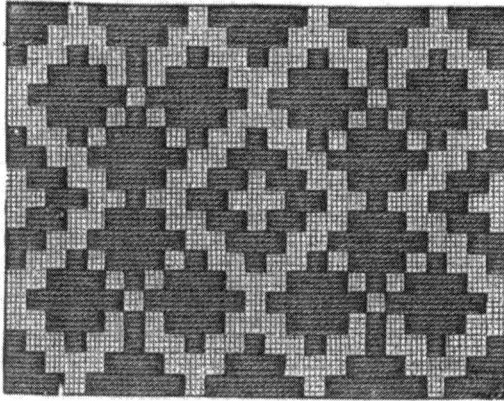

382.—DETAIL OF 380.

the pattern occur in reversed position. Then thread through every double knot of the last row a tassel of 10 strands each 6 inches long, tie them as shown in the illustration, taking in the gold cord; then wind them round with silk and cut the ends even. For No. 368 the strands must be about 24 inches long, and then the pattern is worked like the preceding to the end of the 1st row. 2nd row: Each pattern requires 12 strands * 1 buttonhole knot with the 4th to the 6th, over the 1st to the 3rd strands together, then 1 buttonhole knot with the latter over the former, then 1 buttonhole knot with the 4th to the 6th over the 1st to the 3rd, then 3 buttonhole knots as above with the 7th to the 12th strands; repeat from *. 3rd row: 1 double knot with the 1st to the 3rd and the 10th to the 12th together. Repeat 8 times the 2nd and 3rd rows, letting the double knots occur in reversed position. The remaining strands are drawn together, and others added to form the tassels, which are then wound round as shown in the illustration, and the ends are cut even. Lastly a gold cord is threaded through the knots horizontally and vertically, and carefully fastened.

383.—DETAIL OF 380.

Nos. 369 and 370. Fringes for Furniture, &c. No. 369. Tie along a foundation thread of the required length alternately 2 dark brown and 2 light brown strands of Orient wool folded in half, and work 2 rows of knots in reverse position with 2 threads for each knot. In the 3rd row knot together all the 4 strands of one shade. In the 4th row knot the 4th strand of 1 shade with the 1st of the other, and leave the intervening strands unnoticed. The remaining rows are knotted as is clearly shown in No. 369, but in the last row but 2 the 2 centre strands of each shade are knotted together, tied round with a few strands of the same

335

wool, and all the strands are then tied round with blue wool to form the tassels; then tie some blue wool to the foundation thread, * crochet 11 chain (at the interval shown in the illustration) to the foundation thread, and repeat from *. A tassel of brown and blue wool is then fastened on to each loop of chain, the upper part being sewn over with blue wool as shown in No. 369. For No. 370, tie along a foundation chain of the required length a number of strands of brown wool folded in half, and knot 4 rows in reversed position, then for every vandyke work 6 more knots, divide the strands as shown in the illustration, cross them and tie them with several shades of olive-green wool. For the vandyked border which lies along the upper part of the fringe, tie a strand of olive-green wool to the foundation thread; * (darkest shade) crochet 11 chain; join to the foundation thread and repeat from *. 3 of these loops must lie across 1 vandyke. Then finish each vandyke separately with pale olive wool as follows: join to centre stitch of 1st chain scallop: 5 chain: join to the last of the preceding row; fasten and cut the thread. Then join to each of the lower loops of chain a tassel made with several shades of olive-green wool, and cut the threads even.

INSERTIONS.

For Underlinen—Trimmings—Furniture.

Nos. 371 and 372. Insertions. (Macramé Work.) These two patterns look best when knotted with very fine thread. No. 371 is worked the long way, and is begun by tying double threads, of a yard long, to a double foundation thread. 1st row: Over a doubled horizontal thread, laid across the knotted strands, work 2 buttonhole-knots with every strand. 2nd row: 1 double knot with every 4 strands. 3rd row: Like the 1st row. 4th row: Measure the distances from the illustration, and remember that the strands are numbered according to their *apparent* order in the course of the work. For one diagonal pattern take 6 strands, 3 times alternately place the 6th strand aslant over the 5th, 4th, 3rd, 2nd, and 1st, and work over it 2 buttonhole loops with each of the latter in succession. 5th row: Like the 1st. 6th row: Like the 4th, but in reversed position. 7th to 9th rows: Like the 1st to the 3rd. 10th row: With 16 strands. To form the diamond, place twice alternately the 8th strand diagonally across the other 7, and with the latter work 2 buttonhole loops over the diagonal line; then work the same pattern in reversed position with the 9th to the 16th strands; then with the centre 12 strands, taking the first 3 and the last 3 together, and working with them 1 double knot over the other 6; then 2 patterns in reversed position, according to the illustration. The 4 knotted bars also take 16 strands, 4 to each bar; 6 times alternately 1 buttonhole knot with the 1st and 2nd end together over the 3rd and 4th together, and one buttonhole knot with the latter over the 1st and 2nd. When this row is finished, repeat 9 rows like the first 9, in reversed position. The projecting threads are then fastened on the wrong side and cut off. For No. 372, tie a number of strands to a doubled foundation thread; miss 2 strands, take the 3rd strand and tie it to the foundation thread *before*

384.—WINDOW-BLIND.

the preceding 2 strands, so as to form a loop (working from right to left), and work 14 buttonhole loops over it with the other end of the same thread; then work over the foundation thread 2 buttonhole loops with the 2 threads; repeat so as to form the row of loops shown in the illustration. 1st row: Over a double foundation thread, 2 buttonhole loops, with each strand in succession. 2nd row: 1 double knot with every 4 threads. 3rd

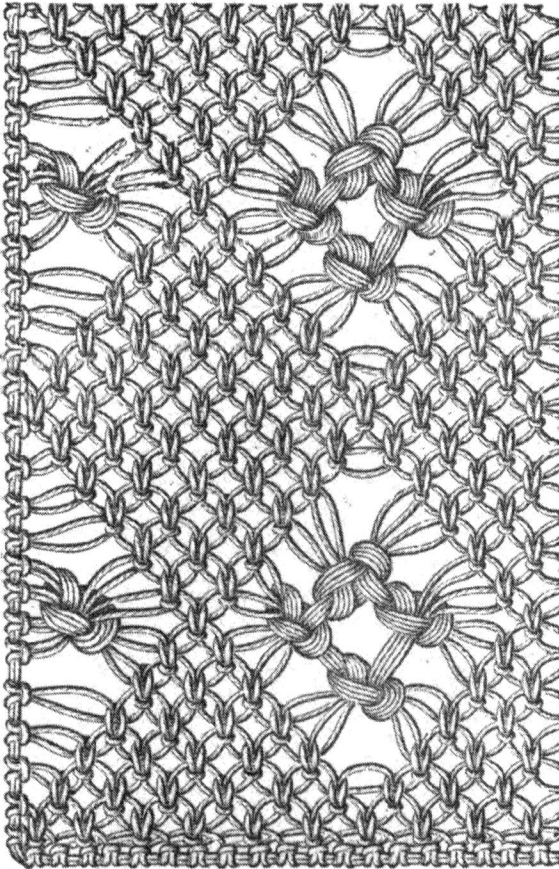

385.—DETAIL OF 384.

row: 4 buttonhole loops, with the 1st over the 2nd, and the 4th over the 3rd of every 4 strands. 4th row: 1 double knot, with the 3rd and 4th end of 1 pattern and the 1st and 2nd of the next. 5th to 7th row: Like the 3rd to the 1st, but in reversed position. 8th row: With 28 strands place the 14th strand diagonally across the 13th to the 1st, and work in succes-

386.—COLLAR (Macramé Work).

387.—WORK-BAG.

sion 2 buttonhole knots over it with each thread; then proceed in the same way, but in reversed position, with the 15th strand placed across the 16th to the 28th; then 12 double

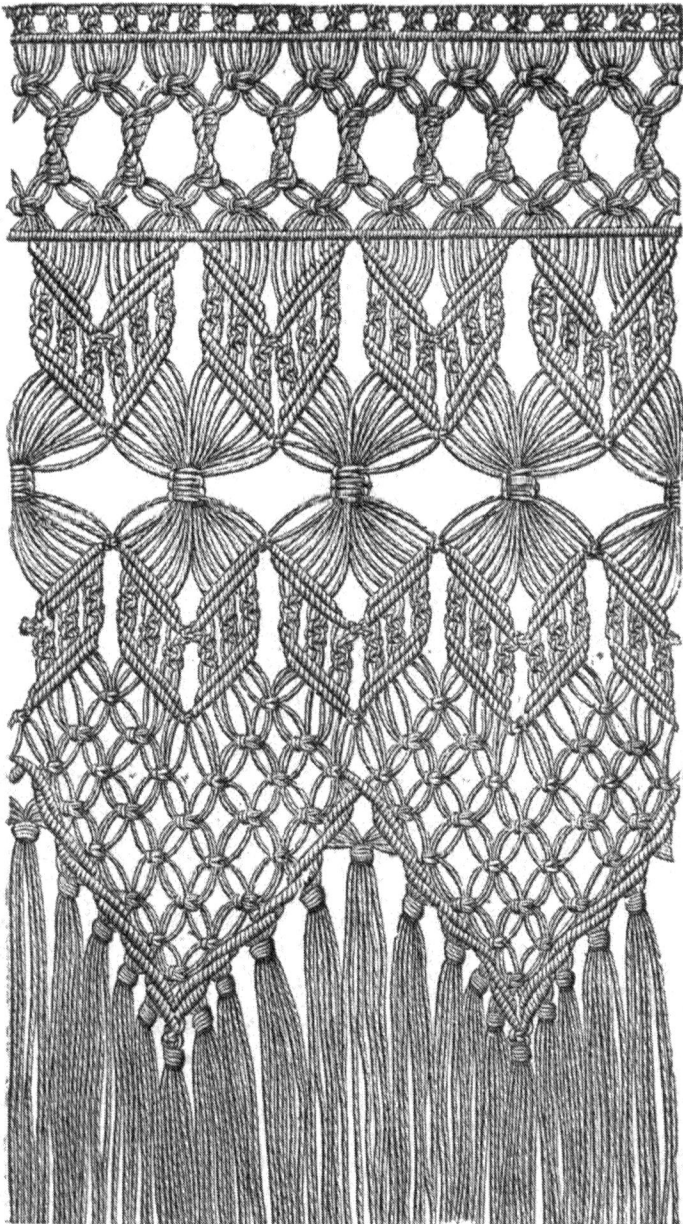

388.—DETAIL OF 387.

knots each with the 3rd to the 6th, the 7th to the 10th, the 11th
to the 14th, the 15th to the 18th, the 19th to the 22nd, and the
23rd to the 26th. These knots are crossed, as shown in the
illustration, and 1 double knot is worked with the 2 last strands
of one and the two first of the following knot. Then work 2
diagonal lines as before, and the square is completed. The 8
rows which follow are like those at the beginning of the pattern;
the projecting threads are then fastened down on the wrong side,
and cut off.

No. 373. Various Purposes. (Macramé Work.) According to
the use for which this is assigned, the insertion may be worked
either in strong silk, thread, or tapestry wool. A number of
strands, about 20 inches long, are folded in half, and knotted
together once. Each of these knots is fastened with a pin to the
weighted cushion, at the distance shown in No. 373. 1st row:
Place a double foundation thread horizontally across the
strands, and work over it 2 buttonhole knots with each strand
in succession. 2nd row; (each pattern requires 4 threads) *, 2
buttonhole knots with the 4th of the first 4 strands over the
centre 2, 2 buttonhole knots with the first strand over the centre
2, repeat from *. 3rd row : Like the first row. 4th row (each
pattern requires 24 strands) : Twice alternately place the first of
the 24 strands aslant over the 2nd to the 12th, and work over it
2 buttonhole knots with each strand in succession, then with the
remaining 12 strands work a similar pattern, but in reverse
position, using the 24th strand as a foundation thread. 5th
row : * 1 raised spot as follows : $4\frac{1}{2}$ double knots, with the 23rd
and 24th strands of 1 pattern, and the 1st and 2nd of the next,
then thread the first of these 4 strands between the 23rd and
24th of the 4th strand, between the 1st and 2nd strands, from
which the $4\frac{1}{2}$ double knots started, draw the strands tight, and
work half a double knot, then, consulting the illustration, place
the 9th, 10th, 11th, and 12th of the 24 strands over the
13th, 14th, 15th, and 16th, and under the 17th, 18th, 19th, and

20th, and place the 5th, 6th, 7th, and 8th strands under the 13th, 14th, 15th, and 16th, and over the 17th, 18th, 19th, and 20th strands, repeat from *. 6th row: Like the 4th, but the pattern must occur in reversed position. 7th to 9th rows: Like the 1st to the 3rd and 10th row, 1 buttonhole knot with the 3rd and 4th strands over the 1st and 2nd, repeat. Then turn back the ends, fasten carefully, and cut them close to the work.

No. 374. Insertion. (Macramé Work.) Our model is knotted with tapestry wool as follows: Fold in half a number of strands 16 inches long, and tie each in a double buttonhole knot, taking of course two doubled strands and making with the first two a buttonhole knot over the last two, and then vice versâ. These knots are then pinned on to a weighted cushion at the distances shown in No. 374, and a double foundation thread is laid across them. 1st row: 2 buttonhole knots with each strand in succession over the foundation. 2nd row: 2 double knots with every 4 strands. 3rd row: Like the 1st. 4th row: * Every 4 of the next 16 strands are put together to form one strand, pass the 3rd of these strands under the 2nd and over the 1st, the 4th over the 2nd and under the 1st, † twice alternately place the 8th end slantwise across the 7th to the 1st and work 2 buttonhole loops with each in succession over the first, then repeat once from †, and then from *. 5th to 8th rows: Like the 3rd and 4th alternately, but the pattern of the even numbered row must occur in reversed position. 9th and 10th rows: Like the 2nd and 1st. 11th row: 1 double buttonhole knot with every 4 strands. The ends are then turned back, and fastened down on the wrong side and cut off close.

No. 375. Insertion. (Macramé Work.) Fold in half a sufficient number of strands of unbleached thread about 16 inches long, taking care that the number is divisible by eight. Then tie together every 4 strands, making a loop with the 3rd and 4th over the 1st and 2nd, and with the 1st and 2nd over the 3rd and 4th. Each loop is then pinned on to a weighted cushion, and a double foundation thread is laid across the

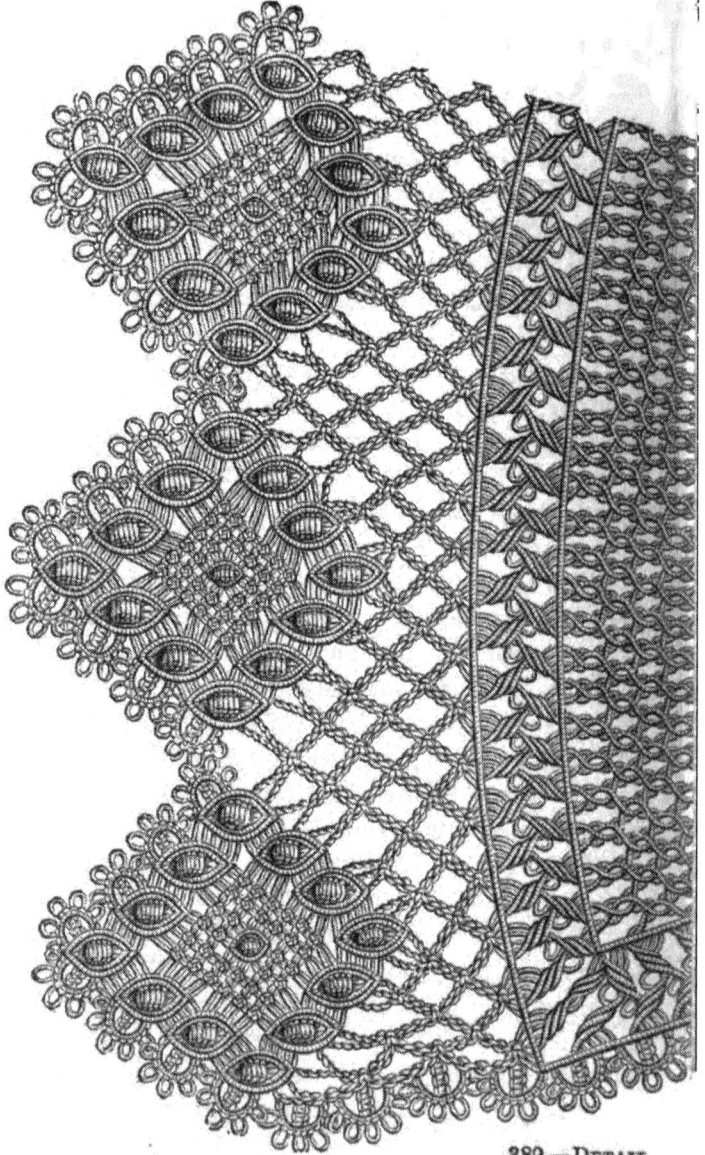

389.—DETAIL

strands. Then work from left to right as follows ;—1st

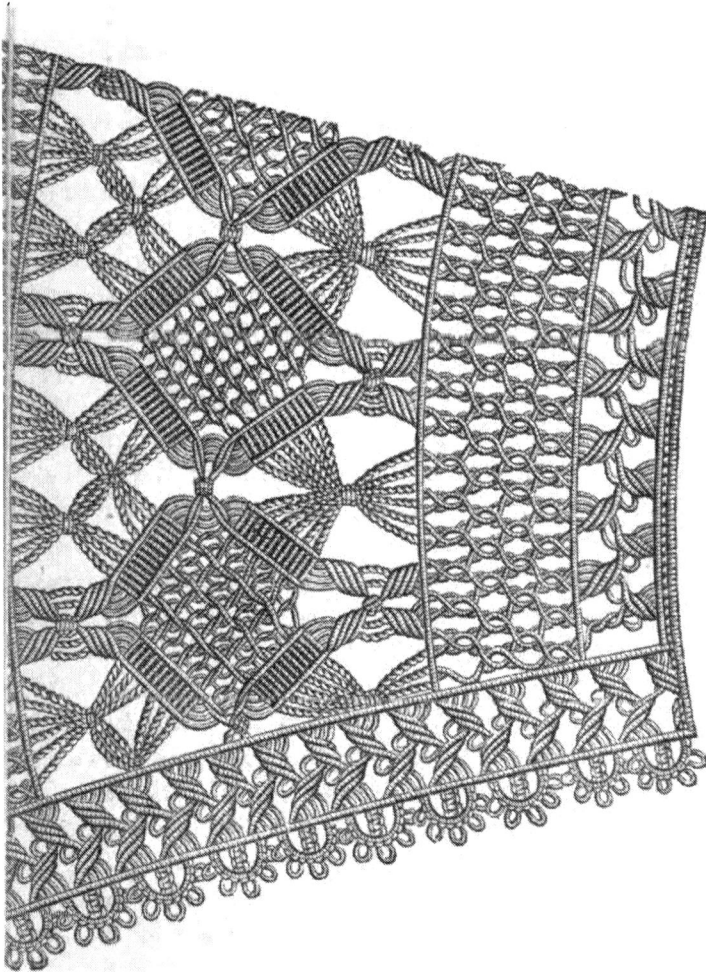

ε

2 buttonhole loops over the foundation thread with every strand in succession. 2nd row: 1 buttonhole loop with the 3rd and 4th of every 4 strands over the 1st and 2nd, and 1 buttonhole loop with the 1st and 2nd over the 3rd and 4th. 3rd row: Like the 1st row. 4th row: * 4 double knots with the 1st to the 4th of the first 16 strands, 3 double knots with the 5th to the 8th, 2 double knots with the 9th to the 12th, and 3 double knots with the 13th to the 16th, repeat from *. 5th row: Leave the first two strands unnoticed, * twice alternately place the 8th of the next 16 strands in a slanting direction across the 7th to the 1st strand, and make 2 buttonhole loops with each of the latter in succession over the 8th strand, twice alternately place the 9th strand in a slanting direction over the 10th to the 16th, and work 2 similar loops with each over the 9th strand, repeat from *. 6th row: Like the 5th, but in reversed position (see illustration as to crossing the strands of each pattern). 7th to 10th rows: Like the 4th to the 1st, but in reversed order of rows. 11th row: Like the 2nd row. Then turn back the 4 strands of every knot, and sew them firmly on the wrong side. The projecting strands are cut away.

No. 376. Insertion for Underlinen. (Knotted Work.) Take 12 strands of thread two yards long and fold them in halves. 1st row: 4 tatted knots with the 1st over the 2nd, the 4th over the 3rd, the 21st over the 22nd, and the 24th over the 23rd; then 1 double knot with the first 4, the centre 4, and the last 4; 4 tatted knots with the 5th over the 6th, and the 20th over the 19th; 3 tatted knots with the 7th over the 8th, and the 18th over the 17th; 1 tatted knot with the 9th over the 10th, and the 16th over the 15th. 2nd row: 2 buttonhole knots with the 11th, 10th, 9th, 8th, 7th, 6th, and 5th strand in succession over the 12th strand, and 2 buttonhole knots with the 14th to the 20th over the 13th. Leave the first and last 4 unnoticed. 3rd to 8th row: Like the preceding, using as foundation thread the strand nearest to the beginning, and the strand used in one row is left

unnoticed in the following one, so that in the 8th row only 2
buttonhole loops are knotted. 9th row: 1 tatted knot with the
1st over the 2nd, and the 24th over the 23rd, 14 tatted knots
with the 4th over the 3rd, and the 21st over the 22nd, 1 purl
between the centre 2 of the 14; then 1 double knot with the
first and last 4 close to the separate tatted knots, so as to form
a loop with each, 2 buttonhole knots with the 6th to the 12th
strand in succession over the 5th, and with the 19th to the 13th
over the 20th, but before knotting this row draw the 5th and
20th strand through the purl of the loop. 10th row: 1 double
knot with the 11th to the 14th strand, 7 times alternately 1
buttonhole knot with the 12th over the 11th, 1 with the 11th
over the 12th, and 1 with the 13th over the 14th strand, then 1
double knot with the 4 centre strands, 15 tatted knots with the
9th over the 10th, and the 16th over the 15th strands, 1 purl
between the 3rd and 4th, 6th and 7th, 9th and 10th, and 12th
and 13th, 20 tatted knots with the 7th over the 8th, and the
18th over the 17th, joining the foundation thread to the nearest
purl after the 4th knot (see illustration), and working 1 purl
between the 6th and 7th, 10th and 11th, 14th and 15th knots,
25 tatted knots with the 5th over the 6th, and with the 20th
over the 19th strand, joining to the purl after the 7th, 13th, and
19th tatted knots, and working 1 purl between the 9th and 10th,
and 15th and 16th, * 7 tatted knots with the 1st over the 2nd,
and with the 24th over the 23rd, 7 tatted knots with the 4th
over the 3rd, and the 21st over the 22nd, joining to the purl
after the 4th knot, 5 double knots with the first and last 4
strands. Repeat once more from *, pass the 4th and 21st strand
through the nearest purls, and work 1 instead of 5 double knots
with the first and last 4 strands. Repeat the 2nd to the 10th
row as often as necessary.

VARIOUS HOUSEHOLD ARTICLES.

Window-Drapery—Towels—Window-Blind—Work-Bag—Basket for Layette—Watch-Pocket.

Nos. 377 to 379. Window-Drapery. Long muslin curtains under curtains of brown rep, which have a border embroidered

390.—EMBROIDERED TOWEL.

on canvas in cross stitch. The design is worked with the following colours:—Etruscan red, yellow, pale blue, light red in wool and filoselle. The rep curtains have also a fringe and tassels of brown wool. White blind of fine holland slightly reeved, and alternating with strips of open knotted work. The lower edge of the blind has a border of the same work above a white fringe. For the knotted work see Illustration 377. Along a double foundation thread tie 34 strands of white cord about two yards

and a quarter in length. 1st row (from left to right): Along
a horizontal cord, 2 buttonhole loops with each strand. 2nd
row: Regulate the interval according to the illustration: 2 buttonhole loops with the 2nd, 3rd, 4th, and 5th strand successively
over the 1st strand, † 5 tatted knots with the next strand over
the 2 following, 5 tatted knots with the next strand but 3 over
the 2nd strand *before* it, joining as shown in the illustration;
repeat 3 times from †, then 2 buttonhole loops over the last

391.—EMBROIDERED TOWEL.

strand with the 33rd, 32nd, 31st, and 30th strands successively.
3rd row: 2 buttonhole loops over the 5th strand with the 4th,
3rd, 2nd, and 1st strands successively, † the next and the next
strand but 4 are left unnoticed, with the 4 strands between;
proceed as follows:—Leave the 2 centre for the foundation and
knot 2 double knots over them with the 1st and 4th; to form
the raised spot join the outside strand of the 4 to the beginning
of the knotted row, pulling through the ends with a crochet-
needle, and knotting 1 double knot close to it; repeat 3 times
349

from †, then 2 buttonhole knots over the 30th strand with the
31st, 32nd, 33rd, and 34th strands successively; repeat the 2nd
and 3rd rows as often as necessary, and finish off with a row like

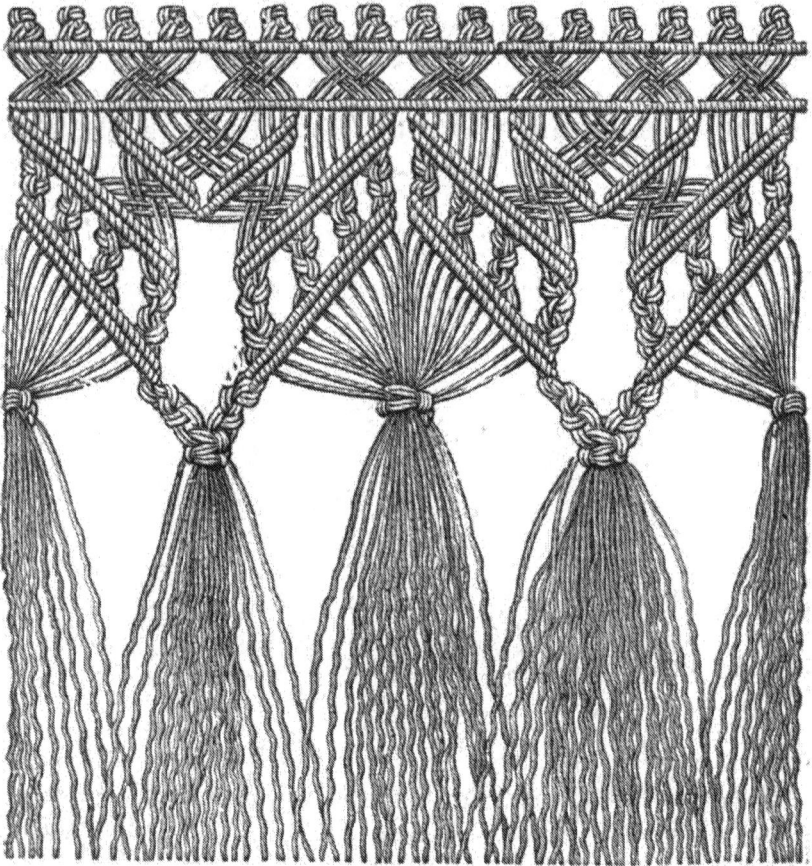

392.—DETAIL OF 390.

the 1st. For the border and fringe see Illustration 379. Knot
8 strands about 2 yards in length to a cord which is passed in
the course of the work through the border, the latter being
worked the narrow way. The beginning of this cord must be on

350

the right side of the border. 1st row (from left to right): 2

393.—DETAIL OF 391.

buttonhole loops over the cord with each of the 16 strands. 2nd

row (right to left): Like the 1st row. 3rd row (left to right):
✝ 5 tatted knots with the 1st strand over the 2nd and 3rd, then

394.—Detail of 391.

with the next strand but 2, 3 tatted knots over the 2 preceding
strands; repeat once more from ✝ 7 double knots with the last 4
strands with 1 double purl between the 1st and 2nd, 3rd and

352

4th, and 5th and 6th.   4th row : † Leave the 1st and 6th strands untouched, 1 raised spot as before with the 4 centre strands ;

395.—Detail of 391.

repeat once more from †.   The last 4 strands are left unnoticed. 5th row : † 3 tatted knots with the next strand over the 2nd next ones, 3 tatted knots with the next strand but 3, over the 2

353   z

preceding. The interval of the foundation cord which forms the scallop must be measured from the illustration; repeat from †. 6th row: Like the 1st row; repeat the 2nd to the 6th row as often as necessary, then join to every scallop of the border 6 strands of 16 inches in length. 1st row: 3 tatted knots with the 1st over the 2nd and 3 with the 4th over the 3rd; repeat. 2nd row: 1 double knot with every 4 strands. 3rd row: Leave the 2 first strands unnoticed, * twice alternately 3 tatted knots with the 1st over the 2nd and the 4th over the 3rd, then with the last 2 of one pattern and the first 2 of the next 1 raised spot; repeat from *. 4th row: 1 double knot with the first 4 of the centre 8 strands, the others left unnoticed. 5th row: 1 raised spot with the centre 4 strands of every pattern, then knot together every 2 strands; see illustration, and cut the fringe even.

Nos. 380 to 383. Towel-Horse and Towel. (Macramé Work). Stand of black polished wood. Towel of coarse cloth worked with red thread according to Illustration 383. Four threads of the ground are required for one stitch. The pattern must be carefully worked, and then the right and wrong sides will be exactly alike. The centre of the border has also a monogram in the same stitch. The pattern given in Illustration 382 may be used instead. The edges of the towel are fringed and knotted in the pattern shown in Illustration 380. Tie every 12 strands in a knot, and before tying the 1st, 7th, and 12th of every division, pass a double strand of blue thread through the work, then divide the 12 strands in half, 4 double knots with every 4 of the 12 white strands, forming purls as shown in the illustration, 4 double knots with each 4 of the centre 8 strands, 4 double knots with the centre 4, then on each side of the pattern, using the white threads for the foundation, and taking in as required, the strands left unnoticed, 24 double knots with the blue threads on each side, consulting the illustration as to forming the purls and measuring the distances.

354

Nos. 384 and 385. Window-Blind. (Macramé.) This pattern, of which No. 385 gives a section in the original size, is begun as follows:—Cut a double foundation thread equal in length to the circumference of the frame and begin at the upper edge, which must measure one-fourth of the whole. Fold a number of strands, 2 yards long, in half, and tie them in the ordinary way to the foundation thread, taking care that the number is divisible by 12. Every pattern takes 24 strands, but the reverse rows begin and end with half a pattern worked with 12 strands. 1st row: Leave the 1st and last 12 strands unnoticed; then 1 double knot with the centre 4 of the next 24 strands; repeat all along the row, and then 1 buttonhole loop with the 1st of the first 12 and 12th of the last 12 over the foundation thread as follows:— Work 1 buttonhole loop from above downward, and then the 2nd from above upward over the foundation thread at the sides of the work. (See No. 385.) These buttonhole stitches are worked in every row. In the 2nd, 3rd, and 4th rows work 2, 3, and 4 double knots with the centre 8, 12, and 16 strands respectively; but in the 2nd row, 1 double knot with the first 4 of the 1st 12 and the last 4 of the last 12. In the 3rd row work the double knot with the 3rd to the 6th of the first 12, and the 7th to the 10th of the last 12. In the 4th row the double knots are worked with the 1st to the 4th and 5th to the 8th of the first 12, and with the 5th to the 8th and the 9th to the 12th of the last 12. 5th row: For one knotted pattern proceed as follows: 1 buttonhole loop with the last 4 strands of one pattern together over the first 4 of the next pattern; then with the latter over the former, 5 double knots with the centre 20 strands; repeat from *. Then 1 double knot with the 3rd to the 6th and the 7th to the 10th of the first and last 12 strands. 6th to the 8th rows: 1 double knot with every 4 strands; but the pattern must occur in reversed position. 9th row: Like the 5th, only that the knotted pattern is worked *after* the double knots. 10th and 11th rows: Like the 4th and 3rd. 12th row: 1 knotted pattern

355

like that of the 5th row with the last 8 strands of one pattern and the first of the next; then a similar knotted pattern with the last 4 of one pattern and the first 4 of the next: continue like the 2nd row. Now repeat as often as necessary the 1st to the 12th row. Then work another row like the first, and one in

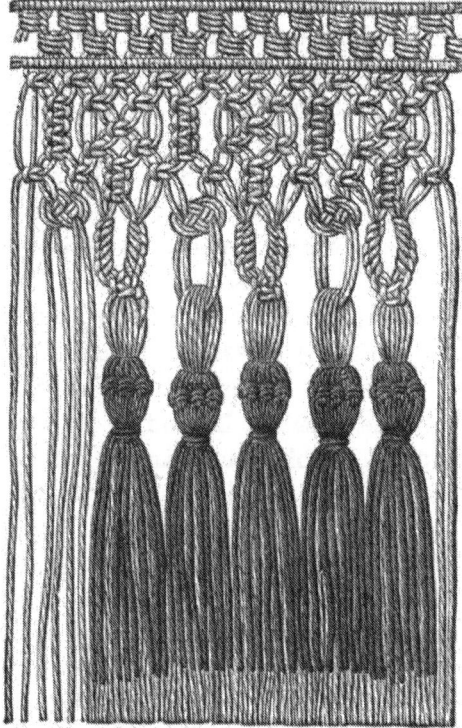

396.—FRINGE FOR TOWEL.

which 2 buttonhole stitches are worked in succession over the foundation thread.

Nos. 386 and 389. Collar. (Macramé Work.) Worked with cream-coloured silk. Tie 159 strands, folded in half, and measuring 2 yards in length, to a double foundation thread about 10 inches long. After tying the strand to the foundation, work close to the knot with 1 strand over the foundation thread a buttonhole knot as follows:—1 buttonhole loop from above downwards and from below upwards, working from right to left. 1st row: 2 buttonhole knots with each strand in succession over a double foundation thread placed close under the first. 2nd row: The intervals must be measured according to the illustration, and the strands numbered in the order in which they occur. With 6 strands, 3 times alternately place the 1st strand aslant over the 2nd to the 6th and work over it 2 buttonhole knots with each strand. In the 3rd repetition of this row work 4 buttonhole knots with the last thread over the strand used as a foundation. 3rd row: Like the preceding, but work the pattern in reversed position with the last 3 strands of one figure and the first 3 of the next, copying the beginning and ends of the rows as shown in No. 389, which gives a section of the collar in the original size, adding new strands as they are required to make the slanting line of the front of the collar. 4th row: Like the 1st row. 5th row: * 4 button-hole loops from below upward with the 1st of the 4 strands over the 2nd, 4 buttonhole loops with the 4th over the 3rd, then 2 buttonhole loops with the 3rd over the 2nd, then 4 buttonhole loops with the 4th over the 2nd, then 4 buttonhole loops with the 2 corresponding strands, 2 buttonhole loops with the 2nd over the 3rd strand; repeat from *. 6th to 8th rows: Like the preceding, but in reversed position, and at the end of the 8th row 2 knotted rows like the first 2 in the 5th row. 9th row: Like the 1st row. 10th row: * 7 chain knots as follows (1 buttonhole loop with the 1st over the 2nd strand, and then with the 2nd over the 1st):—8 chain knots with the 3rd and 4th strands, 9 chain knots with the 5th and 6th strands, 4 times alternately place the 7th strand aslant over the 8th to the 12th and work in succession 2 buttonhole loops over it with each strand, then work a similar pattern in reverse position with the 13th to the 18th strands, then 9 chain knots with the 19th and

20th strands, 8 chain knots with the 21st and 28th strands, 7 chain knots with the 21st and 24th strands; repeat from *.
11th row: * Take 3 strands 1½ yards long folded in half, tie them to the 1st and 2nd of the next 6 strands so as to have 6 new strands there, then 4 double knots with the 1st and 6th strand over the 2nd to the 4th and the 6th new strands, then 5 chain knots with the 7th and 8th strands, 3 chain knots with the 9th and 10th, 1 raised spot as follows :—8 half double

397.—BAG FOR BATHING-DRESS.

knots with the 11th and 14th over the 12th and 13th strands, then take a crochet-needle and draw the strands which have just been used through the place where the 1st of the 8 double knots was tied, and knot the strands tightly close underneath the double knot so as to form the raised spot, 3 chain knots with the 15th and 16th strands, 5 chain knots with the 17th and 18th, then tie on 3 new strands with the 23rd and 24th as described above; repeat from *, but in every repetition except the last work the 4 double knots with the 19th strand of one pattern and the 6th of the next over the 10 strands between and

over the new ones.   12th row : * 6 rows of chain knots with the
first 12 of the 36 strands as follows :—9, 8, 7, and then 3 times
6 chain knots, then 4 times alternately place the 18th strand
aslant over the 17th to the 13th, and work over it 2 buttonhole
loops in succession with each strand, then work the same pattern
in reversed position with the 19th to the 24th, then 6 rows of
chain knots like the former but in reverse order with the 25th

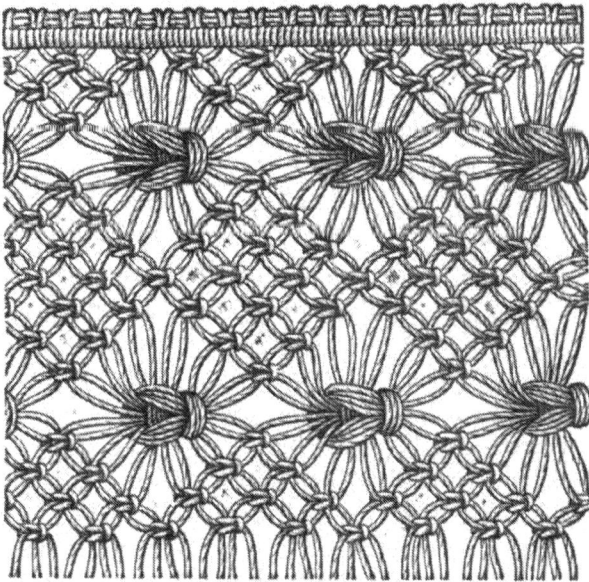

398.—DETAIL OF 397.

to the 36th strand; repeat from *.   13th row ; Place the 13th
strand aslant across the 12th to the 1st and work over it 2
buttonhole loops with each strand, then 12 times place the
next of the first 12 (the 12th first) aslant over the 14th to the 17th
and work over it 2 buttonhole knots in succession with each
strand, then place the 18th strand over the 12 which were used
before as the foundation thread, and work over it 2 buttonhole
knots with each in succession, then work a similar pattern in

reversed position; repeat from *. 14th row: * Twice alternately place the 6th strand over the 5th to the 1st and work over it 2 buttonhole knots with each in succession, then 1 raised spot as before with the 1st and 2nd strand over 2 new short strands tied on as a foundation, then twice alternately place the 1st strand over the 2nd to the 6th and work over it 2 buttonhole loops with each strand, then knot a similar pattern in reversed position with the 31st to the 36th, and work the raised spot with the last 2 strands of one pattern and the first 2 of the next, but not until the first knotted row of the 2nd pattern has been worked; then consult the illustration, and by its help and that of the description already given work the centre pattern of the principal figure. The next 13 rows are like the first 13 but in reverse order; the rows of chain knots in the 16th to the 18th rows must be worked according to the illustration, and the last 4 rows must be continued to form the front of the collar, adding new strands as required by the shape. The 2 strands added to the lower edge of the border in the last row must be knotted just after the 6th strand has been tied; they consist of 1 strand of a yard long folded in half, and are tied with 2 buttonhole loops over the foundation threads. 28th row: * 1 double knot with every 8 strands, using the centre 4 as a foundation, then 2 chain knots with the first 4, taking in 2 at a time, 2 chain knots with the last 4, taking in 2 at a time; repeat from *. 29th and 30th rows: Like the preceding, but the pattern must occur in reversed position, and at the beginning of the 30th row, after having worked the double knot of the 3rd and 4th patterns, and then always after the double knot of the 5th and 6th patterns, 2 rows of chain knots 4 in each row, and 2 knots with every 2 strands. 31st row: * For a medallion pattern. With the centre 12 of 48 strands. Place the 24th strand over the 25th to the 30th and work over it 2 buttonhole loops with each strand, place the 25th over the 23rd to the 19th and work over it 2 buttonhole loops with each strand, the 24th over the 26th

to the 30th and work over it 2 buttonhole loops with each
strand, the 26th over the 23rd to the 19th and work over it 2
buttonhole loops with each strand, then with the 8 strands
which have *not* been used as foundations 1 raised spot, then the
last strand used as a foundation over the next 5, and work 2
buttonhole loops over it with each strand, then the corresponding
strand is placed over the next 5, and 2 buttonhole loops worked
with each strand, then a similar knotted row, and, lastly, a
similar row with the corresponding strand on the other side,
which completes the medallion. Continue the pattern of the
28th and 30th rows with the remaining strands, and repeat
from *. The following rows, as may be seen from the illustration, are the same as the medallion patterns and the first rows
of the border. The pattern inside the squares formed by the
medallions is only rows of double knots in reversed position
with a medallion in the centre. The row of purls round the
border is worked as follows:—* 6 buttonhole knots with the
first of 8 strands over the 2nd with 1 purl between the 2nd and
3rd and 4th and 5th. The purls are made by working the
buttonhole stitch a little way off the preceding and then pushing
it close up, then $2\frac{1}{2}$ double knots with the 3rd and 8th strand
over the intervening ones, then these 6 strands placed by
the one used before as a foundation and 6 buttonhole knots
worked over them with 1 purl before the 1st and between the
2nd and 3rd and 4th and 5th; these knots must be tied very
tight, so that the foundation does not seem too thick. Lastly,
turn back the 8 strands on the wrong side of the work and cut
off the projecting strands.

Nos. 387 and 388. Work-Bag (Macramé Work). Dark red
plush bag, lined with silk of the same colour, hemmed and
drawn up with a silk cord of the same colour. The macramé
trimming is knotted from the pattern given in No. 388 with
écru-coloured purse silk. Fold in half 162 strands of silk about
2 yards long and knot them to a double foundation thread tied

in a circle. 1st round : 1 double knot with every 4 strands. 2nd round : A double foundation thread is laid across the strands, close under the knots, 2 buttonhole knots with every strand in succession over the foundation thread. 3rd round : 1 double knot with every 8 strands, using the centre 4 as a foundation. 4th round : 8 half double knots with the last 4 of one pattern and the first 4 of the next, using the centre 4 of these 8 strands as a foundation. 5th and 6th rounds : Like the 3rd and 2nd. 7th round : Every pattern requires 18 strands. * Twice alternately place the 1st strand across the 2nd to the 9th and work over it 2 buttonhole knots with each strand

399.—BASKET FOR LAYETTE.

in succession, then work a similar pattern, but in reversed position, with the 10th to the 17th, then 1 double knot with the centre 4 of the 18 strands; repeat from *. 8th round : 1 double knot with every 3 strands, using only 1 strand as a foundation. 9th round : Like the 7th. 10th round : 3 double knots with the last 9 of 1 pattern and the first 9 of the next, using the centre 16 as a foundation. 11th to 13th rounds : Like the 7th to the 9th. 14th round : Every pattern requires 36 strands, and takes in the last 9 of the 1st pattern and the first 9 of the next but one ; * 1 double knot with the 7th, 8th,

362

9th, 10th, 11th, and 12th strands, and with the 25th, 26th, 27th, 28th, 29th, and 30th, using the centre 4 as a foundation, then

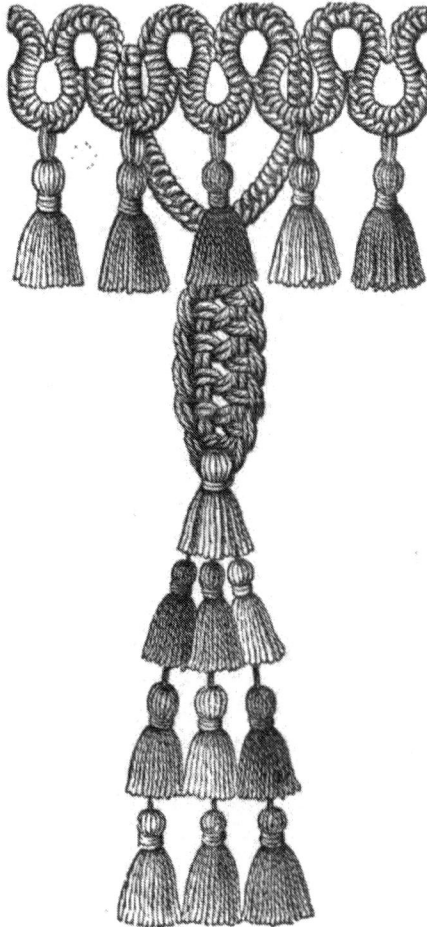

400.—DETAIL OF 399.

1 double knot with the 4th, 5th, 6th, 7th, 8th, and 9th, the 10th to the 15th, the 22nd to the 27th, and the 28th to the 33rd, using 2 strands as a foundation, then 6 times 1 double knot

with the next 6 of the same 36 strands, using 4 strands as a foundation: repeat from *. 15th round: * 5 separate double knots with the centre 30 of the 36 strands, using 2 strands as a foundation, then 4 separate double knots with the centre 24,

401.—WATCH-POCKET.

using 4 as a foundation, then 3 separate double knots with the centre 18, using 2 as a foundation, then 2 separate double knots with centre 12 strands, using 4 as a foundation, then 1 double knot with centre 6 strands, using 2 as a foundation; repeat from *. 16th round: For the outline of every vandyke * place

the last 2 strands of one pattern over the first of the next, and
work over them 2 buttonhole loops with each of the 6 in succession, then place the 3rd and 4th strand over the 5th and 6th,
and work with the latter 2 buttonhole knots in succession, 2
buttonhole knots with the first foundation strands, and with the
7th to the 9th over 3rd and 4th, then place the 8th and 9th
strands over the 10th to the 12th, and work 2 buttonhole knots

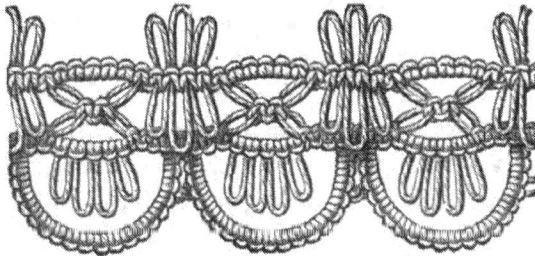

402.—DETAIL OF 401.

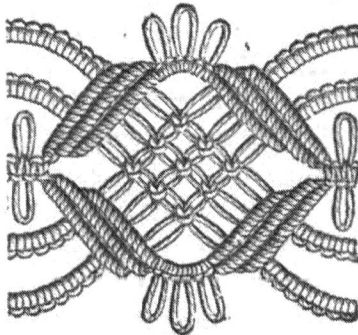

403.—DETAIL OF 401.

with them and with the former foundation strands, and with
the next 3 strands over the 8th and 9th, and so on to the end of
the vandyke. The other half of the outline is worked in the
same pattern, but in reverse order, as shown in No. 388. 1
double knot is worked with the centre 6 strands at the end of
each vandyke, using 4 strands as a foundation; repeat from *.

Then knot the remaining strands to form the fringe as shown in the illustration, adding fresh strands when necessary.

Nos. 390 and 392. Towel. (Cross Stitch, Holbein and Knotted Stitch.) Towel of coarse white linen, with an embroidered border and knotted fringe at each end. When the pattern is worked, the towel is hemmed at each end, and the fringe is knotted with coarse white thread as follows. (No. 392.) A number of strands of about 24 inches long are folded in half, and knotted together two and two, by making a knot with the 2nd and 3rd strand over the 1st and 2nd, and then with the 1st and 2nd over the 2nd and 3rd. (See No. 392, which represents a pattern of the fringe in the original size.) The knots are then fastened to the weight cushion with pins in a straight line. Close underneath the knots arrange a double foundation thread, and work the 1st row from left to right as follows : 2 buttonhole knots, with each strand over the foundation thread. 2nd row: Like the preceding, but consulting the illustration, and tying together every 8 strands, by taking the 5th and 6th under the 4th and 3rd and over the 1st and 2nd, then the 7th and 8th over the 4th and 3rd and under the 1st and 2nd. 3rd row: Each pattern takes 32 strands, and the spaces must be measured from the illustrations, the strands being numbered according to the order in which they come in the work. * Knot the centre 8 of the 32 strands in the manner we described above, and then twice alternately carry the 9th end aslant across the 10th to the 16th, and work over it 2 buttonhole loops in succession with each strand, then work a similar pattern in reversed direction with the 17th to the 24th strands, then 2 buttonhole loops with the 16th over the 17th strand, plait the 9th to the 16th strands as above described, twice alternately carry one strand over the 2nd to the 16th, and work over it 2 buttonhole loops with each in succession, then work a similar pattern in reverse position with the 17th to the 32nd, repeat from *. 4th row: With every 4 strands, twice alternately 1 buttonhole loop with the 1st

366

and 2nd together, over the 3rd and 4th, and then with the latter over the former. 5th row : * Twice alternately carry the 1st end aslant over the 2nd to the 32nd, and tie with each in succession 2 buttonhole knots over it, then a similar pattern with the 17th to the 32nd, then with the 13th to the 16th, and the 17th to the 20th, work a row like the 4th row, but 3 instead of 4 double knots, then with the same 8 strands, 2 double knots with the 1st, 2nd, 7th, and 8th over the rest, but after the first double knot, take in 5 new strands, and tie them to the foundation thread and round the last double knot, then double knot with the last 12 of one pattern and the first 12 of the next, using the centre 8 as a foundation, then knot together the 1st, 2nd, 11th, and 12th on the wrong side, cut the strands even, and wind them lightly round a fine knitting-needle to make them curl.

Nos. 391, 393—396. Towel (Embroidery and Macramé Work). Coarse holland towel, embroidered with coloured cotton and white thread, and finished off at each end with knotted fringe. Trace the design upon the holland, and embroider the design as shown in Nos. 393 to 395 in chain, overcast, feather, knotted, and buttonhole stitch, filling up the figures in herring-bone, plain, and lace stitch. The outlines are worked with cotton, and the filling up put in with white thread. When the embroidery is finished, unravel about 4 inches of the holland at each end for the fringe, and knot it as follows :—1st row : Place a double foundation thread across the strands, and tie over it 2 buttonhole knots with each strand in succession. 2nd row : 3 buttonhole knots with every 4th strand over the preceding 3 strands. 3rd row : Like the 2nd row, but in reversed position. 4th row : Like the 1st row. 5th row : 1 double knot with every 4 strands. 6th row : Leave the first 2 strands unnoticed. * 4 double knots with the 1st to the 4th of the first 12 strands, 1 double knot with the 5th to the 8th, 1 double knot with the 9th to the 12th, 1 double knot with the 7th to the 10th, 1 double knot with the 5th to the 8th, 1 double knot with the 9th

Macramé Lace.

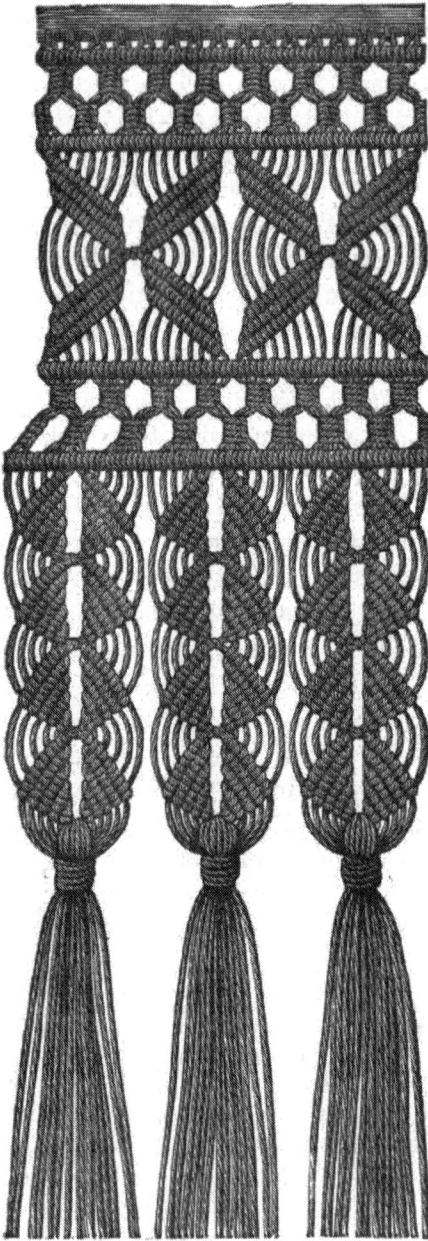

404.—DETAIL OF 405.

368

405.—CRAVAT.

406.—TIE, WITH FRINGE.

to the 12th; repeat from *.   7th row: * 1 double knot with

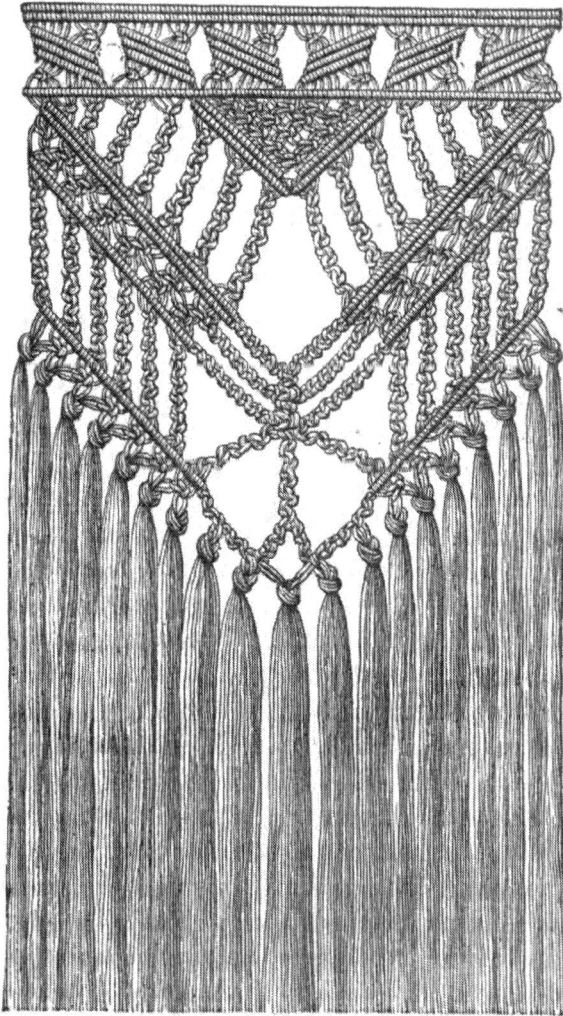

407.—DETAIL OF 406.

the 1st to the 4th strand, 1 double knot with the 5th to the
8th, 3 double knots with the 9th to the 12th; repeat from *

8th row : Leave the first 2 strands unnoticed. * 1 Josephine knot with the 1st to the 4th of the first 12 strands, twist the strands a short distance below (see No. 396), then thread 6 strands folded in half through the loop to form a tassel, add 5 double threads of blue cotton, tying them round in separate knots, and then winding blue thread round all the strands together and cutting the tassels even.   Lastly, 6 buttonhole knots with the 5th over the 6th to the 8th strands, and 6 with the 12th over the 9th to the 11th strands ; tie the centre 2 of these 8 strands, add 4 fresh strands as above, and tie 1½ double knot round them, and finish with a tassel like the one described above.

Nos. 397 and 398. Bag for Bathing Dress (Knotting, Crochet, and Netting). The bag itself is of brown leather, and is covered with a pattern knotted in macramé work with fine string. The sides are covered with netting, and so is the upper part, which is drawn up with cord and tassels. The handles also have large tassels on each side of the bag. For the macramé work proceed as follows :—Along a foundation chain of the required length knot a number of strands 2 yards long, folded in half, and fasten the work to the weighted cushion. Over a double thread placed horizontally across the strands (see No. 398) knot the first row : 2 buttonhole loops with each strand in succession over the horizontal thread. 2nd row (it takes 12 strands for a pattern) : 1 double knot with the centre 4 of every 12 strands ; these double knots consist of a right and a left knot as follows :— Hold fast the centre 2 strands which serve as a foundation with the third and fourth fingers of the left hand : for the left knot, place the first strand loosely over the foundation threads towards the right so that it makes a loop to the left, and hold it between the thumb and forefinger of the left hand. Then pass the fourth strand over the first and back again through the loop ; it must go under the foundation threads, and upward through the loops. Lastly, draw the knotted threads close together ; the right knot is made in the same way, but in reversed order. 3rd row (for the space to be left consult No. 398): 1 double knot with the 3rd, 6th, and the 7th to 10th of every 12 strands. 4th row: 1 double knot with the 1st to 4th, the 5th to 8th, and the 9th to 12th of every 12 strands. 5th row: The first 2 and the last 2 strands are left unnoticed, 1 double knot with the 3rd and 4th strands of 1 double knot, and the 1st and 2nd of another; repeat. 6th to 8th row: Like the 4th to the 2nd row. 9th row: The first 6 and the last 6 remain unnoticed, 1 double knot with the last 6 of one pattern and the first 6 of the next, using the 4 centre strands as a foundation; repeat the 2nd to the 9th row as often as necessary, but the last row of all must be like the 1st instead of the 9th, then cut off and fasten the projecting ends. The sides of the work form the upper end of the bag, and a horizontal thread is laid across them, over which a row of double crochet is worked which takes in the knotted strands at the same time. The macramé work and netting are then sewn on to the leather bag, as shown in No. 397.

Nos. 399 and 400. Basket for Layette (Macramé Work). Shallow, oblong basket of osier work, draped outside with blue cashmere, and edged round with macramé fringe and tassels. The cashmere is cut on the straight and must be 12 inches wide and the length required by the basket; it is then arranged in pleated scallops, as shown in Illustration 399. The macramé work round the upper edge is knotted with ivory silk as follows: Fasten on to a weighted cushion 4 strands of silk, each about 3 yards long; leave the 4th strand unnoticed, and * knot 12 buttonhole loops with the 1st strand over the 2nd and 3rd strands for a foundation; then leave the 1st strand and knot 16 buttonhole loops with the 4th strand over the 3rd and 2nd; repeat from *. The smaller scallops form the upper edge of the border. Small tassels of ivory silk are tied to the lower scallops, as shown in Illustration 400. Also, according to the same illustration, join to ends folded in half to the 1st and 4th connecting cord, and for the left half of the scallop, knot 18 buttonhole loops with the 1st strand over the 2nd, 3rd, and 4th; and for the right half, 18 similar loops with the 4th over the 1st, 2nd, and 3rd. Then join the foundation threads, knot 1 double over the 6 foundation threads, using the 1st and 8th strand to work with. In the first 2 double, use only the centre 4 as foundation threads, and the 1st and 2nd and 7th and 8th to work with. Then * join the 8 strands, placing the 1st and 2nd in a loop under the 3rd to the 6th, then the 7th and 8th under the 1st and 2nd, and over the 5th and 6th; then again under the 1st and 2nd and over the 3rd and 4th, through the 1st loop; draw it up slightly and repeat 3 times from *. Then 3 double, as at the beginning of this pattern, and tie the ends

408.—DETAIL OF 410.

together, adding tassels of different coloured silks, as shown in

Illustration 400. The layette is lined inside with blue cash-mere.

409.—DETAIL OF 411.

410.—WORK-BAG.

411.—SIDE-POCKET.

Nos. 401 to 403. Watch-Pocket (Knotted Work). Pocket of claret-coloured satin with knotted work of écru-coloured thread. For the puffings of the front use claret-coloured satin,

with rows of insertion in knotted work between each. The back
of the pocket is of satin quilted in diamonds, and finished off
with silk cord and small silk buttons. The wrong side of the
pocket is cut out of cardboard, covered with claret-coloured
silk. A metal ring crocheted round with claret-coloured purse
silk is used to hang up the pocket, and the sewing on is hidden
by loops of silk cord and tassels, arranged as shown in the
illustration. For the knotted insertion (see Illustration 403)
proceed as follows:—Along a double foundation thread knot
8 threads which have been folded in half, and so make 16 ends.
1st row: Pass the 8th end over the first 7, and use it for a
foundation thread. Working from right to left, knot 2 buttonhole loops with each thread. Then proceed in the same way
from left to right with the 10th to the 16th end, using the 9th
as the foundation. The strands of thread will always be
numbered according to their position in the row which is being
knotted. 2nd and 3rd row like the preceding one. Then follow
2 inserted rows. In the first of these 1 double knot is to be
knotted out of the centre 4 strands of the 16, measuring the
intervals according to the illustration. In the 2nd inserted
row 1 double knot is knotted out of the centre 8 strands—that
is, 1 double knot out of each 4 strands. 4th row: Use the 2nd
strand as a foundation and work with the 1st strand * 2 tatted
knots (these knots consist of a buttonhole loop from above to
below, and a second buttonhole loop from below to above the
foundation), 3 times alternately 1 purl, 1 tatted knot, then 1
tatted knot, then use the 15th end as a foundation, and repeat
with the 15th from *, then 1 double knot with each 4 of the
centre 12. Then follow 2 inserted rows as before, but in reverse
order. 5th to 7th rows: Like the 1st to 3rd, but in reverse
order (see illustration). 8th row: With the 1st strand over the
2nd and 3rd as foundation, and with the 16th over the 15th
and 14th, 14 tatted knots each, with the 4th strand over the
5th and 6th, and with the 13th strand over the 12th and 11th,

9 tatted knots each, with the 7th strand over the 8th and with the 10th over the 9th 2 buttonhole loops each, then 2 double knots with the 2 centre 4 strands; twice alternately 1 double purl, 2 double knots, then with the 7th over the 8th strand, and with the 10th over the 9th 2 buttonhole loops each. Repeat the 1st to the 8th rows till the required length is knotted, fasten on new thread as often as required by means of a weaver's knot. For the lace (see Illustration 402) as follows :—Knotting the narrow way, knot 5 strands on to a double foundation, so that they make 10 strands. 1st row: 1 double knot with the first 4 strands on the left side, 1 double purl, 2 double knots as follows :—1 double knot with the 5th and 10th strands over the 6th, 7th, 8th, and 9th, then with the 9th over the 8th 20 tatted knots, inserting a purl between the 17th and 18th, which is joined to the scallop of the following row, 2 double knots with the 5th and 10th strands over the 6th and 7th. 2nd row: 5 tatted knots with the 1st strand over the 2nd, 5 tatted knots, 1 purl between each, with the 8th over the 7th strand, 2 double knots with the 3rd and 6th over the 4th and 5th strands at the interval shown by the illustration. 3rd row: 2 double knots with the 1st and 4th strands over the 2nd and 3rd, 3 double knots with a double purl between each, then 1 double knot, 2 double knots with the 5th and 8th over the 6th and 7th strands, 2 double knots with the 5th and 8th strands over the 6th, 7th, 8th, 9th, and 10th, 20 tatted knots with the 10th over the 9th strand, joining after the 3rd knot to the scallop in the previous row, and inserting 1 purl between the 17th and 18th knots, 2 double knots with the 5th and 8th over the 6th and 7th strands. Repeat the 2nd and 3rd rows till the required length is knotted.

ARTICLES OF DRESS, WORK-BAG,
ETC., ETC.

Cravats with Macramé Fringe—Work-Bag—Side-Pocket—Hanging
Work-Case.

Nos. 404 and 405. Cravat (Macramé Work). Navy blue
satin cravat, with a knotted fringe of navy blue purse silk. The
cravat should be 4 inches wide, and 32 doubled strands of silk
are knotted along each end. With these 64 strands proceed as
follows (from left to right) :—1st row: Over a double thread
laid across the strands, 2 buttonhole loops with every strand in
succession. 2nd row : With every 4th strand, 4 buttonhole
loops over the 3 preceding strands. 3rd row : Like the preceding, but in reversed position. At the beginning and end of
this row work 4 buttonhole stitches with the 2nd over the 1st,
or the last over the last but one. 4th row : Like the 1st row.
5th row : The strands are numbered as they appear in the course
of the work. (See No. 404.) * (With 16 strands for 1 leaf
pattern) place the 1st strand slantwise across to the 8th and
work over it 2 buttonhole loops with each ; repeat from * ; and
then, with a similar pattern in reversed position with the 9th to
the 16th strand, using the 16th strand as the foundation, then
2 buttonhole stitches with the 8th strand over the 9th, then
another leaf pattern with the 1st to the 8th strand, in the same
position as that with the 9th to the 16th, and then another with
the 9th to the 16th strand like that with the 1st to the 8th.
6th to 9th row : Like the first 4, but in the 9th row, between
the 1st and 2nd strand and between the last and last but one,
knot with buttonhole loops 2 double strands, so that there are
8 single strands in the following row. 10th row : * (With 10
strands) for a triangular pattern, 5 times alternately pass the
6th strand over the 1st, and work over it 2 buttonhole loops

with each strand, decreasing in each row by 2 loops, and then a triangle in reversed position with the 7th over the 12th strand, then 2 buttonhole stitches with the 6th over the 7th; repeat 3 times from *, then take the 1st to the 6th and the 7th to the 12th strand, and tie them close to the last row. (See No. 404.) Pass 8 strands about 4 inches long above the loop between the knotted pattern, and tie them round like a tassel; repeat 5 knots from *. Cut the ends even.

Nos. 406 and 407. Cravat with Macramé Fringe. Blue silk ribbon scarf with a knotted white silk fringe, for which proceed as follows: Along a double foundation thread knot 30 strands folded in half. 1st row : Place a double thread across the strands, and work over it 2 buttonhole loops with each strand. The strands will be numbered as they appear in the course of the work. 2nd row (see Illustration 407) : 1 double knot with the 7th to the 10th strand, * place the 1st strand diagonally across the 10th and work over it 2 buttonhole loops with each strand ; * repeat twice, then 1 double knot with the 1st to the 4th ; repeat 5 times from *; the three last repetitions must be in reversed position. 3rd row : Like the 1st row. 4th row : 1 double knot with the first 4 of the centre 20 strands, then 4 double knots with the centre 16, 3 double knots with the centre 12, 2 with the centre 8, 1 with the centre 4, * place the 20th end across the 30th, and work over it 2 buttonhole knots with each ; repeat once with the 19th strand from the last *, then the 41st and 42nd strands over the 40th to the 28th, and work 2 similar rows in reversed position. 5th row : Leave the first and last 2 strands unnoticed (see illustration), 6½ chain knots with the 27th to the 30th, and with the 31st to the 34th, then 6 chain knots with the 23rd to the 26th, and the 35th to the 38th, then 5½ chain knots with the 39th to the 42nd.

Nos. 408 and 410. Work-bag, of Plush. Bag of claret plush, drawn up with thin silk cord and tassels, and ornamented with knotted work of écru thread. Ruchings, bows and ends of claret satin ribbon are then added, as shown in No. 410. For the macramé work have ready a sufficient number of strands, about one yard long, and folded in half. Make a loop with the 3rd and 4th over the 2nd and 1st, and then a loop with the 1st and 2nd over the 3rd and 4th. Each knot so made is

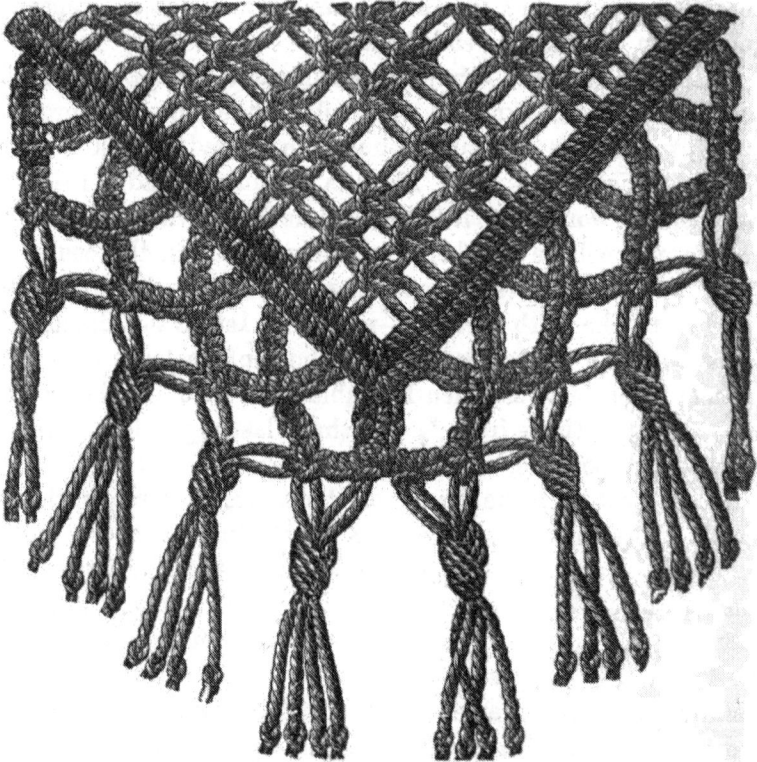

412.—DETAIL OF 411.

fastened with a pin on to the macramé cushion, so that they form a straight line. Then place a double foundation thread close under the knots across the strand, and work from left to right. 1st row: 2 buttonhole loops, with each strand over the foundation thread. 2nd row: * With every 4 strands, 2 buttonhole knots with the 3rd over the 4th, 2 buttonhole knots with the 2nd over the 3rd, 2 buttonhole knots with the 1st over the 2nd, repeat from *. 3rd row: Like the 1st row, but in this and the 5th row 3 more strands about 24 inches, folded in half, must be

413.—HANGING WORK-CASE WITH KNOTTED FRINGE.

taken; and in the course of the 4th, 6th, 7th, 8th, and 9th rows two such strands must be taken, and the requisite knots to be worked with them, as shown by the pattern, while in the 11th to the 15th rows the same number must be left out. 4th row: Every pattern requires 24 strands, the spaces must be measured from the illustration, and the strands are numbered according to their apparent orders in the course of the work. * 5 times alternately with the 1st and 2nd strands together, 1 buttonhole knot over the 3rd and 4th, 1 buttonhole knot with the 3rd and 4th over the 1st and 2nd, then a row of knots like the preceding, with the 5th to the 8th and the 9th to the 12th, twice alternately place the 13th strand aslant over the 14th to the 18th, and work over it 2 buttonhole knots with each strand (14th to 18th) in succession; then with the 13th to the 15th and the 16th to the 18th half a knot each, using the centre strand as a foundation, then twice alternately place the 13th strand aslant over the 14th to the 18th, and work two buttonhole loops with each in succession over it; then work a similar pattern with the 19th to the 24th strands, and repeat from *. 5th row: Like the 1st. 6th row: (16 strands to a pattern) * twice alternately place the 6th strand aslant over the 5th to the 1st, and work over it 2 buttonhole loops, with each in succession; then knot a similar pattern in reversed position with the 11th to the 16th, twenty times alternating 1 buttonhole knot with the 7th and 8th over the 9th and 10th, and 1 knot with the 9th and 10th over the 7th and 8th, repeat from *. 7th row: 1 double knot with the 4th and 5th and 12th and 13th strands (taken respectively 2 together) over the 6th and 11th strands, and over the 7th to the 10th in the knotted row of this pattern; then using the 4 centre strands as a foundation, 2 double knots with the 14th to the 16th strands of this pattern, and the 1st to the 3rd of the next. 8th row: Twice alternately place the 1st strand aslant over the 2nd to the 6th, and work over it 2 buttonhole loops with each strand; then a similar figure with the 16th to, the 11th strand, but in reversed position. 9th row (see No. 408): Like the 7th, but only one double knot instead of two. 10th to 13th rows: Like the 6th to the 9th. 14th to 16th rows: Like the 6th to the 8th. 17th to the 21st row: Like the 5th to the 1st. 22nd row: Take the 1st and 2nd strands together, and work 1 buttonhole loop over the 3rd and 4th, and then do the same with the 3rd and 4th over the 1st and 2nd. Lastly: Fasten the threads on the wrong side, and cut off the projecting strands.

Nos. 409, 411, 412. Side-Pocket. (Knotted Work.) Pocket of black grosgrain silk, 7 inches long in the longest part, and 5 wide. A strong steel clasp closes the pocket, with tassels at each end. The chain which suspends the pocket to the waistband is knotted in the pretty Josephine knot. The knotted work is begun with the flap as follows :—Take a length of cord measuring 6 inches for the foundation, and tie to it at intervals lengths of 36 inches folded in half. Then proceed as follows :— 1st row : Along a horizontal cord knot 2 buttonhole loops with each end of cord. 2nd row : 1 double knot with 4 ends of cords ; repeat 3rd and 4th rows : Like the 1st. 5th row : Leave unnoticed the first 2 and the last 2 ends during the next 9 rows. Divide the remaining ends into eights. Form 1 double knot with the centre four of each eight. 6th row : 1 double knot with the first 2 and the last 2 of each eight, consulting the illustration to see the length of cord which must be left between the knots. 7th row : Like the 5th ; repeat 7 times the 5th to the 7th rows, tatting knot with the 4th end over the 3rd. In the second 4 and the last 4 but one, only 4 tatted knots can be formed instead of 5. Then join these knotted fours at the beginning and end with a double knot, and join on 2 ends at the centre scallops at the point of the flap, join the 4 ends together in a knot to form the fringe, and cut the ends even. The pocket front is knotted in the same way, increasing the number of ends as required by size of pattern.

Nos. 413 to 415. Hanging Work-Case with Knotted Fringe. The pocket itself is cut out of blue grosgrain silk and batiste écru. On the flap is a monogram between two broad straps of batiste and knotted work edged with fringe. A metal ring crocheted round with silk cord is attached to smaller similar rings on the pocket by means of cord and tassels, and serves to hang it to the wall of the dressing-room or study. The cords and tassels are of blue silk, and the batiste on each side of the knotted work is arranged in puffings. For the knotted work, which is done the narrow way, see Illustration 415. Along a double foundation thread of écru twist join 12 threads folded in half,

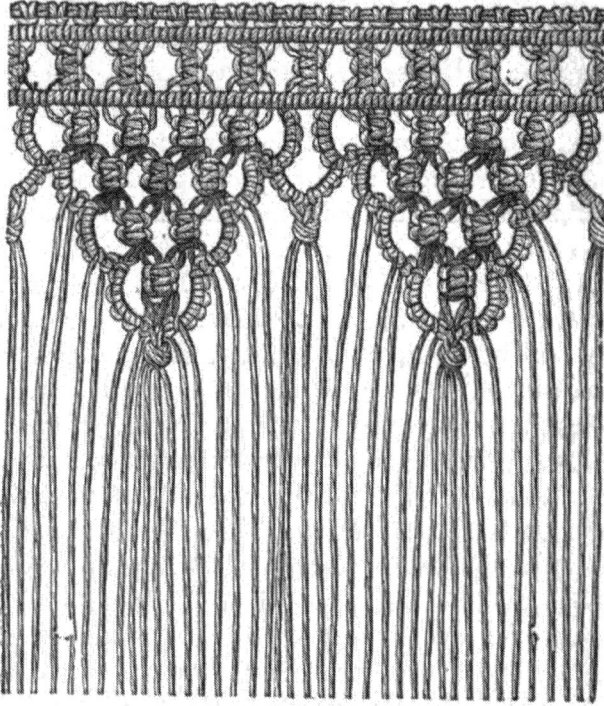

414.—DETAIL OF 413.

and measuring rather more than 2 yards. With these 24 strands work as follows the 1st row: Work from left to right over a double foundation thread 2 buttonhole loops with each strand one after the other. 2nd row: With the first 4 of the 24 strands 3 double knots; repeat. 3rd row: Like the 1st row. 4th row: With the 1st to the 4th strand and with the 21st to the 24th strand 8 double knots, with the centre 16 strands 4 raised spots. For each of these work 3 double knots with the next 4 strands in succession, and then join to the 2 knotted strands where the illustration shows. To do this draw the thread through with a crochet hook and work 1 double knot on the right side of the work. 5th row : With the centre 12 strands 3 raised spots as before, with the 5th and 6th and the 19th and 20th 5 double buttonhole knots each, then with the 1st over the 2nd, and the 24th over the 23rd end 1 buttonhole loop, with the 3rd to the 6th and with the 19th to the 22nd 1 double knot each. 6th row : With the centre 8 strands 2 raised spots, with the 7th and

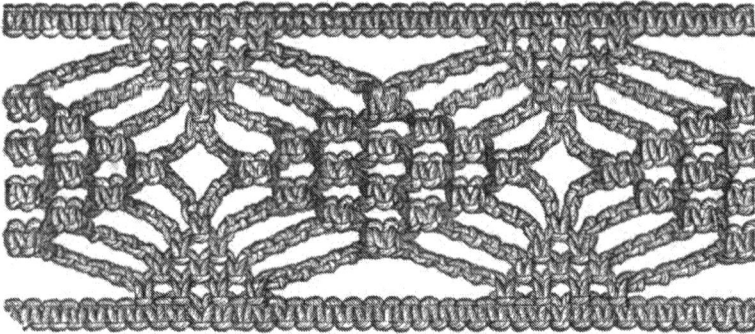

415.—DETAIL OF 413.

8th and with the 17th and 18th 4 double buttonhole loops each, with the 1st to the 4th and with the 5th to the 8th, with the 17th to the 20th and with the 21st to the 24th 1 double knot each. 7th row : With the centre 4 ends 1 raised spot, with the 9th and 10th and with the 15th and 16th strands 3 double button-hole knots each, with the 3rd to the 6th and with the 7th to the 10th strands, with the 15th to the 18th and the 19th to the 22nd strands 1 double knot each, with the 1st over the 2nd and the 24th over the 23rd 1 buttonhole loop each. 8th row : With the 11th and 12th and with the 13th and 14th strands 2 double buttonhole knots each, then with all the 24 strands 1 double

knot with every 4, with the 11th and 12th and the 13th and
14th 2 double buttonhole knots each. 9th to the 11th rows :
Like the 7th to the 5th rows, but in reverse order, then repeat
the 4th to the 11th row as often as required, knotting 12
instead of 6 double knots in every repetition of the 4th row
with the first and last 4 strands. The new pieces of thread are
tied on in a weaver's knot. For the fringe see Illustration 414.
It is worked the long way over a double foundation chain with
folded strands of about 2 yards long. The first 3 rows are like
the first 3 of the insertion, except that in the 2nd row 2 instead
of 3 double knots are to be worked. 4th row : Every pattern
requires 20 strands, 4 raised spots are knotted with the 16
centre strands, with the 1st over the 2nd and the 20th over the
19th 3 tatted knots each. With the centre 12 ends of a pattern
3 raised spots, with the 2nd over the 3rd and the 19th over the
18th 2 buttonhole knots each, then with the 3rd over the 4th
and the 18th over the 17th 4 tatted knots, with the 2nd over
the 1st and the 19th over the 20th $2\frac{1}{2}$ tatted knots, then with
the 20th and the 1st strand of the following pattern 1 double
buttonhole knot, after which knot together the 19th and 20th
and the 1st and 2nd strands of the next pattern. 6th row :
With the centre 8 strands of a pattern 2 raised knots, with the
4th and 5th and 17th and 18th 2 buttonhole knots, then with
the 5th and 6th and 15th and 16th strands, 4 tatted knots. 7th
row : With the centre 4 strands 1 raised spot, with the 6th and
7th and the 15th and 14th 2 buttonhole loops each, then with
the 7th and 8th and 14th and 13th 4 tatted knots each, with
the 8th and 7th and 13th and 12th 2 buttonhole loops each,
and then the centre 4 ends in 1 knot. At the lower edge the
strands are cut to an equal length, and the fringe is sewn on
to the insertion with overcast stitches.

LONDON,
Warwick House, Dorset Buildings,
Salisbury Square, E.C.

New Books and New Editions

PUBLISHED BY

WARD, LOCK, & CO.

FOR FAMILY READING AND REFERENCE.

TWO HUNDRED AND SIXTY-FIFTH THOUSAND,
New Edition, post 8vo, half-bound, price 7s. 6d.; half-calf, 10s. 6d.

Mrs. BEETON'S
BOOK OF HOUSEHOLD MANAGEMENT,

Comprising every kind of Practical Information on Domestic Economy
and Modern Cookery, with numerous Woodcuts and Coloured Illustrations.

"Mrs. Isabella Beeton's 'Book of Household Management' aims at being a compendium of household duties in every grade of household life, from the mistress to the maid-of-all-work. It is illustrated by numerous diagrams, exhibiting the various articles of food in their original state, and there are also coloured plates to show how they ought to look when dished and ready for the table. The verdict of a practical cook of great experience, on returning the book to her mistress, was, 'Ma'am, I consider it an excellent work; it is full of useful information about everything, which is quite delightful; and I should say anyone might learn to cook from it who never tried before."—*The Athenæum.*

Second Edition, price One Guinea, cloth gilt, and gilt edges;
or in Two Volumes, 25s.

BEETON'S GREAT BOOK OF POETRY.

From Cædmon and King Alfred's Boethius to Browning and Tennyson. Containing nearly Two Thousand of the Best Pieces in the English Language. With Sketches of the History of the Poetry of our Country, and Biographical Notices of the Poets. Presenting a Collection of Poems never before gathered together within the limits of a Single Volume.

Four Hundred English Poets are represented in this Volume. A separate Collection of American Poems, with Biographies, is added to these. Thus, in one book, a view of the Growth and Changes of the English Language, as seen in its Highest Developments, is possible. Not less than a Thousand Volumes have been examined in order to form a selection worthy to receive respect and regard from all Lovers of the Divine Art of Poesy.

Published by Ward, Lock, and Co.

New Books and New Editions.

Enlarged, corrected, and revised to the latest date.

THE DICTIONARY OF UNIVERSAL INFORMATION,

of Geography, History, and Biography. Containing 23,000 Distinct Articles, 12 Large Coloured Maps, and 110 Separate Tinted Plates of Views and Portraits.

Just ready, Vol. I.—A to H—containing 59 separate Tinted Plates and 7 large Coloured Maps—Africa, North America, South America, Asia, Australia, China, and Europe. Demy 8vo, 836 pp., cloth gilt, price 10s. 6d.

" This work is a marvel of condensation, containing in comparatively small compass a perfect m ine of information, under the three great heads of Geography, History, and Biography. The seven Maps in the (first) volume are admirably executed."—*Leeds Mercury*, January 24, 1877.

In Two Vols., price 21s., half-bound, the Revised and Enlarged Edition, newly Illustrated by 128 full-page and 1,500 smaller Engravings.

BEETON'S SCIENCE, ART, AND LITERATURE: A Dic-

tionary of Universal Information; comprising complete Summary of the Moral, Mathematical, Physical, and Natural Sciences; a plain Description of the Arts; an interesting Synopsis of Literary Knowledge, with the Pronunciation and Etymology of every leading term. The work has been with great care Revised, Enlarged, and newly Illustrated.

⁂ There is no volume extant comparable to this for the amount of information compressed into a small space. Amongst works on Technical Science and Information, there is no volume that can be more safely recommended to teachers, students, or practical men, than Beeton's Scientific Dictionary.

Half-bound, 7s. 6d.; half-calf, 10s. 6d., copiously Illustrated.

BEETON'S DICTIONARY OF NATURAL HISTORY: A

compendious Cyclopædia of the Animal Kingdom. Illustrated by upwards of 200 Engravings.

Plainly written and carefully illustrated information upon the Animal Kingdom is entitled to rank high amongst the aids to knowledge, and we believe that the present work will materially assist readers and students in following their examination of Comparative and Human Physiology, as well as give the answers to every-day questions in Natural History.

Half-bound, price 7s. 6d.; half-calf, 10s. 6d.

BEETON'S DICTIONARY OF BIOGRAPHY: Being the Lives

of Eminent Persons of all Times. With the Pronunciation of every Name. Illustrated by Portraits, Engraved after Original and Authoritative Pictures, Prints, &c. Containing in all upwards of Ten Thousand Distinct and Complete Articles.

This BIOGRAPHICAL DICTIONARY contains, in the most compact form possible, and within a compass of some 700 or 800 pages, an account of the Lives of Notable and Eminent Men and Women in all epochs. The Portraits, printed on tinted paper, are faithfully reproduced from original or authoritative sources. These Engravings form a totally new feature in BEETON'S BIOGRAPHICAL DICTIONARY, none having appeared in the First Edition.

Published by Ward, Lock, and Co.

MOXON'S POPULAR POETS.

Edited by WILLIAM MICHAEL ROSSETTI.

Crown 8vo, elegant cloth gilt, gilt edges, 3s. 6d.; morocco antique, 7s. 6d.; ivory enamel, 7s. 6d.; morocco, extra, 10s. 6d.; tree calf, 10s. 6d.

The press and the public, alike in Great Britain and her Colonies, and in the United States, unite in their testimony to the immense superiority of Messrs. Moxon's Popular Poets over any other similar collections published by any other house. Their possession of the copyright works of Coleridge, Hood, Keats, Shelley, Wordsworth, and other great national poets, places this series above rivalry. Upwards of 100,000 volumes have already been sold.

1. BYRON'S POETICAL WORKS.
2. LONGFELLOW'S POETICAL WORKS.
3. WORDSWORTH'S POETICAL WORKS.
4. SCOTT'S POETICAL WORKS.
5. SHELLEY'S POETICAL WORKS.
6. MOORE'S POETICAL WORKS.
7. HOOD'S POETICAL WORKS.
8. KEATS' POETICAL WORKS.
9. COLERIDGE'S POETICAL WORKS.
10. BURNS' POETICAL WORKS.
11. TUPPER'S PROVERBIAL PHILOSOPHY.   The Four Series complete.
12. MILTON'S POETICAL WORKS.
13. CAMPBELL'S (THOMAS) POETICAL WORKS.
14. POPE'S POETICAL WORKS.
15. COWPER'S POETICAL WORKS.
16. HUMOROUS POEMS.
17. AMERICAN POEMS.
18. MRS. HEMANS' POEMS.
19. THOMSON'S POEMS.
20. A SELECTION OF MISCELLANEOUS POEMS.
    In the Press.
21. HOOD'S POETICAL WORKS.   Second Series.

MOXON'S LIBRARY POETS.

The complete and continuing success of Moxon's Poets, in the popular Three-and-Sixpenny Series, has induced the House to publish a Library Edition of Moxon's Poets, price Five Shillings per volume. Handsomely printed on good paper, either half Roxburgh or cloth, gilt edges. The Entire Series of the Popular Poets is now included in this issue.

E. Moxon, Son, & Co., Dorset Buildings, Salisbury Square.

The Haydn Series of Manuals.

Demy 8vo, in 1 thick vol. cloth, 18s.; half calf, 24s.; full caff, or tree calf, 31s. 6d.

HAYDN'S DICTIONARY OF DATES, relating to all Ages and Nations; for
Universal Reference. Fifteenth Edition. Revised and greatly Enlarged by
BENJAMIN VINCENT, Assistant-Secretary of the Royal Institution of Great
Britain; containing the History of the World to Autumn 1876.

"The most universal book of reference in a moderate compass that we know of
in the English language."—*Times.*

"It is by far the readiest and most reliable work of the kind for the general
reader within the province of our knowledge."—*Standard.*

Demy 8vo, cloth, 18s.; half calf, 24s.; full calf, or tree calf, 31s. 6d.

HAYDN'S DICTIONARY OF POPULAR MEDICINE AND HYGIENE, comprising all possible Self-Aids in Accidents and Disease; being a Companion
for the Traveller, Emigrant, and Clergyman, as well as for the Heads of Fami-
lies and Institutions. Edited by the late EDWIN LANKESTER, M.D., F.R.S.,
Coroner of Central Middlesex. Assisted by distinguished Members of the
Royal College of Physicians and Surgeons.

Demy 8vo, cloth, price 18s.; full calf, 31s. 6d.

HAYDN'S UNIVERSAL INDEX OF BIOGRAPHY. From the Creation to the
Present Time. For the Use of the Statesman, the Historian, and the Jour-
nalist. Containing the chief events in the lives of eminent persons of all ages
and nations, arranged chronologically and carefully dated; preceded by the
Biographies and Genealogies of the chief Royal houses of the world.

Demy 8vo, cloth, price 18s.; full calf, 31s. 6d.

HAYDN'S DICTIONARY OF THE BIBLE. For the Use of all Readers and
Students of the Holy Scriptures of the Old and New Testaments, and of the
Books of the Apocrypha.

Demy 8vo, cloth, price 18s.

HAYDN'S DICTIONARY OF SCIENCE. Comprising Astronomy, Chemistry,
Dynamics, Electricity, Heat, Hydrodynamics, Hydrostatics, Light, Magnet-
ism, Mechanics, Meteorology, Pneumatics, Sound and Statics; preceded by
an Essay on the History of the Physical Sciences.

E. Moxon, Son, & Co., Dorset Buildings, Salisbury Square.

Crown 8vo, cloth gilt, 7s. 6d.
EASTERN LIFE, PRESENT AND PAST. By Harriet Martineau. New Edition, with a new Preface recently written by the Author (probably her last literary work), with full-page illustrations.

"'Eastern Life, Present and Past,' exhibits the history and generation of the four great faiths—the Egyptian, the Jewish, the Christian, and the Mohammedan —as they appear when their birthplaces are visited in succession. The work in which she gave out her views on her return ranks on the whole as the best of her writings; and her reputation assumed a new, a graver, and a broader character after its appearance."—*Daily News*, June 29, 1876.

Crown 8vo, cloth gilt, thick paper, with plates, 5s.
DANA'S SEAMAN'S MANUAL. Containing a Treatise on.Practical Seaman--ship, with plates; A Dictionary of Sea Terms; Customs and Usages of the Merchant Service; Laws Relating to the Practical Duties of Masters and Mariners. By R. H. Dana, jun., Author of "Two Years Before the Mast." Revised and corrected in accordance with the most recent Acts of Parliament. By John J. Mayo, Esq., Registrar-General of Shipping and Seamen.
"This is a book for all time."—*Star of Gwent.*

Fcap. 8vo, cloth, 2s. 6d.
GREENWOOD'S (COLONEL) HINTS ON HORSEMANSHIP TO A NEPHEW AND NIECE. The Wood Engravings, photographed from life, are illustrative of the management of the reins in accordance with the principles enunciated in the work.

Crown 8vo, cloth gilt, 5s.
HEAP OF STONES. By S. Holden.

Fcap. 8vo, cloth, 5s.
HOUGHTON'S (LORD) PALM LEAVES.

Fcap. 8vo, cloth, 5s.
HOUGHTON'S (LORD) MEMORIALS OF MANY SCENES.

Fcap. 8vo, cloth gilt, 2s. 6d.
ICH DIEN. A Poem.

Fcap. 8vo, cloth gilt, 3s. 6d.
KELLET RIGBYE, THE POETICAL WORKS OF. 256 pages.

Fcap. 8vo, wrapper, 1s.
RESURGENS. A Poem, by the Author of "Ich Dien."

Crown 8vo, cloth gilt, 5s.
RHYMES OF AN EDITOR, including "Almost." By Henry Morford, Author of "Rhymes of Twenty Years."

New Volume of Poems.
Crown 8vo, cloth gilt, 3s. 6d.
POETICAL DEBRIS. By George Messinger.

E. Moxon, Son, & Co., Dorset Buildings, Salisbury Square.

Thomas Hood's Works.

HOOD'S WORKS. Complete in 10 vols. All the Writings of the Author of the "Song of the Shirt" ("Hood's Own," First and Second Series, included). With all the original Cuts by Cruikshank, Leech, &c. A complete re-issue. In 10 vols., crown 8vo, cloth, 50s.; half calf, 70s.; half morocco, 70s.

COMPLETE EDITION OF HOOD'S POETICAL WORKS IN TWO VOLUMES.

1. **HOOD'S SERIOUS POEMS.** A New and Complete Edition, with full-page Illustrations. Crown 8vo, cloth gilt, 5s.

2. **HOOD'S COMIC POEMS.** A New and Complete Edition, with full-page Illustrations. Crown 8vo, cloth gilt, 5s.

*** *These two volumes contain the entire poems of the late* THOMAS HOOD, *which are now collected and issued complete for the first time.*

HOOD'S OWN; or, Laughter from Year to Year. First and Second Series in one vol., complete, with all the original Illustrations by Cruikshank, Leech, &c. In entirely new and handsome binding. Now ready, new edition. Royal 8vo, cloth gilt, 10s. 6d.

HOOD'S OWN; or, Laughter from Year to Year. First Series. A new edition. In one vol. 8vo, illustrated by 350 Woodcuts. Cloth plain, 7s. 6d.; gilt edges, 8s. 6d.

HOOD'S OWN. Second Series. In one vol., 8vo, illustrated by numerous Woodcuts. Cloth plain, 7s. 6d.; gilt edges, 8s. 6d.

HOOD'S POEMS. Twentieth Edition. In one vol., fcap. 8vo cloth plain, 5s.

HOOD'S POEMS OF WIT AND HUMOUR. Sixteenth Edition. In one vol., fcap. 8vo, cloth plain, 3s. 6d.

HOOD'S WHIMS AND ODDITIES. In Prose and Verse. With 87 original designs. A new edition. In one vol., fcap. 8vo, cloth plain, 3s. 6d.

HOOD'S WHIMS AND ODDITIES & WIT AND HUMOUR. With 87 original designs. In one vol., fcap. 8vo, 6s.

E. Moxon, Son, & Co., Dorset Buildings, Salisbury Square.

S. O. Beeton's National Reference Books,

FOR THE PEOPLE OF GREAT BRITAIN AND IRELAND.

The Cheapest and Best Reference Books in the World.

Each Volume complete in itself, and containing from 512 to 590 Columns.
Price 1s. in strong cloth binding.

Beeton's British Gazetteer : A Topographical and Historical Guide to the United Kingdom. Compiled from the Latest and Best Authorities. It gives the most Recent Improvements in Cities and Towns; states all the Railway Stations in the Three Kingdoms, the nearest Post Towns and Money Order Offices.

Beeton's British Biography : From the Earliest Times to the Accession of George III.

Beeton's Modern Men and Women : A British Biography from the Accession of George III. to the Present Time.

Beeton's Bible Dictionary. A Cyclopædia of the Geography, Biography, Narratives, and Truths of Scripture.

Beeton's Classical Dictionary : A Cyclopædia of Greek and Roman Biography, Geography, Mythology, and Antiquities.

Beeton's Medical Dictionary. A Safe Guide for every Family, defining with perfect plainness the Symptoms and Treatment of all Ailments, Illnesses, and Diseases. 592 columns.

Beeton's Date Book. A British Chronology from the Earliest Records to the Present Day.

Beeton's Dictionary of Commerce. A Book of Reference. Containing an Account of the Natural Productions and Manufactures dealt with in the Commercial World ; Explanations of the principal Terms used in, and modes of transacting Business at Home and Abroad.

Beeton's Modern European Celebrities. A Biography of Continental Men and Women of Note who have lived during the last Hundred Years, or are now living.

Beeton's Ready Reckoner. A Business and Family Arithmetic. With all kinds of New Tables, and a variety of carefully digested Information, never before collected. Cloth, 1s.

Beeton's Sixpenny Ready Reckoner. 96 pages.

Price One Shilling each.

Beeton's Guide Book to the Stock Exchange and Money Market. With Hints to Investors and the Chances of Speculators.

Beeton's Investing Money with Safety and Profit.

Beeton's Complete Letter-Writer, for Ladies and Gentlemen. Containing: The most approved Love Letters—Applications for Employment—Replies to Advertisements—Answers to Invitations—Requests to execute Commissions—and Letters respecting Domestic Affairs, Visits, and Education ; also Brief Complimentary Notes—Forms for the Address, Commencement, and Conclusion of Letters, and useful Hints regarding Letter-Writing generally. 8vo, 1s.

Beeton's Complete Letter-Writer for Ladies. 6d.

Beeton's Complete Letter-Writer for Gentlemen. 6d.

Published by Ward, Lock, and Co.

Handsome Presentation Volumes.

Now Ready, price 10s. 6d., a New Volume by HENRY SOUTHGATE, Author of
" Many Thoughts of Many Minds," "Musings About Men," &c.

Noble Thoughts in Noble Language: A Collection of Wise and
Virtuous Utterances, in Prose and Verse, from the Writings of the Known Great
and the Great Unknown. With an Index of Authors. Compiled and Analytically
Arranged by HENRY SOUTHGATE, Author of " Many Thoughts of Many Minds,"
"Musings About Men," " Woman," &c. &c.
*This Volume will especially recommend itself to those who can appreciate and
value the best thoughts of our best writers.*

Price One Guinea, exquisitely bound, cloth gilt and gilt edges, the Best Books ever
produced in Colours, and eminently fitted for Presents.

The Fields and the Woodlands, Illustrated by Painter and Poet.
Consisting of Twenty-four Pictures, printed in the highest style of Chromographic
art, by LEIGHTON Brothers. With Verses of character and beauty appropriate
to the Pictures. Printed on thick toned paper.

Price One Guinea, uniform with the above.

Pictorial Beauties of Nature. With Coloured Illustrations by
Famous Artists. This magnificent book forms a Companion Volume to " The
Fields and the Woodlands," and the splendid collection of Twenty-four Pictures
is unrivalled by anything ever brought together within the bounds of a single
volume.

In One handsome Volume, cloth gilt, 15s.; elegantly bound in bevelled boards,
gilt edges, price 21s.

Dalziel's Illustrated Arabian Nights' Entertainments. With
upwards of 200 Pictures drawn by J. E. MILLAIS, R.A., J. TENNIEL, J. D.
WATSON, A. B. HOUGHTON, G. J. PINWELL, and T. DALZIEL, together with
Initial Letters, Ornamental Borders, &c., engraved by the Brothers DALZIEL.

Beautifully bound in cloth gilt, price 7s. 6d.; in bevelled boards, gilt edges,
price 10s. 6d.; in morocco, price 21s.

Dalziel's Illustrated Goldsmith. Comprising " The Vicar of Wake-
field," " The Traveller," " The Deserted Village," " The Haunch of Venison,"
" The Captivity: an Oratorio." " Retaliation," "Miscellaneous Poems," " The
Good-Natured Man," " She Stoops to Conquer," and a Sketch of the Life of
Oliver Goldsmith by H. W. DULCKEN, Ph.D. With 100 Pictures, drawn by G.
J. PINWELL, engraved by the Brothers DALZIEL.

Handsomely bound in cloth, gilt sides and edges, price 21s.

Old English Ballads. Illustrated with 50 Engravings from Drawings
by JOHN GILBERT, BIRKET FOSTER, FREDERICK TAYLER, JOSEPH NASH, GEORGE
THOMAS, JOHN FRANKLIN, and other eminent Artists.

Fcap. 4to, cloth, gilt side, back, and edges, price 21s.

Christmas with the Poets. A Collection of Songs, Carols, and
Descriptive Verses relating to the Festivals of Christmas, from the Anglo-Norman
Period to the Present Time. Embellished with 53 Tinted Illustrations by BIRKET
FOSTER. With Initial Letters and other Ornaments printed in Gold, and with
Frontispiece in Colours.

Published by Ward, Lock, and Co.

BOOKS FOR BOYS.

Beeton's Boys' Own Library.

⁎⁎The best set of Volumes for Prizes, Rewards, or Gifts to English Lads. They have all been prepared by Mr. Beeton with a view to their fitness in manly tone and handsome appearance for Presents for Youth, amongst whom they enjoy an unrivalled degree of popularity, which never flags.

Coloured Plates and Illustrations, price 5s. cloth; or cloth gilt, gilt edges, 6s.

1. **Stories of the Wars.** TILLOTSON. From the Rise of the Dutch Republic to the Death of Oliver Cromwell.
2. **A Boy's Adventures in the Barons' Wars**; or, How I won My Spurs. J. G. EDGAR.
3. **Cressy and Poictiers.** J. G. EDGAR.
4. **Runnymede and Lincoln Fair.** J. G. EDGAR.
5. **Wild Sports of the World.** J. GREENWOOD.
6. **Curiosities of Savage Life.** By the Author of "Wild Sports of the World."
7. **Hubert Ellis.**
8. **Don Quixote.** CERVANTES. 300 Illustrations.
9. **Gulliver's Travels.** By Dean SWIFT.
10. **Robinson Crusoe.** By DANIEL DEFOE.
11. **Silas the Conjurer.**
12. **Savage Habits and Customs.** By the Author of "Wild Sports of the World."
13. **Reuben Davidger.** J. GREENWOOD.
14. **Brave British Soldiers and the Victoria Cross.**
15. **Zoological Recreations.** By W. J. BRODERIP, F.R.S.
16. **Wild Animals in Freedom and Captivity.**
18. **The World's Explorers.** Including Livingstone's Discoveries and Stanley's Search.
19. **The Man among the Monkeys**; or, Ninety Days in Apeland. Illustrated by G. Doré.
20. **Golden America.** By JOHN TILLOTSON.

NEW BOOKS FOR BOYS.

Ice World Adventures; or, Voyages and Travels in the Arctic Regions. From the Earliest Period to the English Expedition of 1875. By JAMES MASON. With 48 full-page and other Illustrations. Crown 8vo, cloth gilt, 5s.

Lion Hunting; or, Adventures and Exploits in India, Africa, and America. By JULES GERARD. Crown 8vo, cloth gilt, gilt edges, 5s.

Antony Waymouth; or, The Gentlemen Adventurers. By W. H. KINGSTON. Crown 8vo, cloth gilt, 3s. 6d.

Published by Ward, Lock, and Co.

Beeton's Boys' Prize Library.

NEW PRESENTATION VOLUMES FOR BOYS.

1,088 pages, 8vo, with numerous Engravings, full-page and in the text, cloth gilt, price 5s. ; gilt edges, 6s.

3. **BEETON'S BRAVE TALES, BOLD BALLADS, AND** TRAVELS BY SEA AND LAND. *Containing:* Historical Stories— Hubert Ellis—Ingonyama—Highland Regiments as they Once Were—King of Trumps—Scientific Papers—Silas the Conjurer—Sports and Pastimes— Victoria Cross Gallery—The Zoological Gardens, &c.

Cloth, plain edges, 5s. ; gilt edges, 6s.

4. **BEETON'S TALES OF CHIVALRY, SCHOOL STORIES,** MECHANICS AT HOME, AND EXPLOITS OF THE ARMY AND NAVY. A Book for Boys. Illustrated by separate Plates and numerous Woodcuts inserted in the Text.

Cloth, plain edges, 5s. ; gilt edges, 6s.

5. **BEETON'S HERO SOLDIERS, SAILORS, & EXPLORERS,** Gymnastics, Telegraphy, Fire Arms, &c. 1,088 pages, with 50 full-page Engravings on toned paper, and numerous Woodcuts.

Cloth, plain edges, 5s. ; gilt edges, 6s.

6. **BEETON'S FAMOUS VOYAGES, BRIGAND ADVEN-** TURES, TALES OF THE BATTLE-FIELD, &c. Illustrated by sepa- rate Plates and numerous Woodcuts inserted in the Text.

Just Ready, Uniform with the above, cloth, plain edges, 5s.; gilt edges, 6s.

7. **BEETON'S VICTORIOUS ENGLISH SEA STORIES,** TALES OF ENTERPRISE, and SCHOOL LIFE. Illustrated by sepa- rate Plates and numerous Woodcuts inserted in the Text.

The Young Ladies' Library.

With Illustrations. Handsomely bound in cloth gilt, price 2s. 6d.

1. **Sunshine and Rain; or,** Blanche Cleveland. By A. E. W.

2. **Roses and Thorns ; or, Five** Tales of the Start in Life.

3. **Bible Narratives ; or, Scrip-** ture Stories. By the Rev. FREDE- RICK CALDER, M.A.

4. **Pleasure and Profit ; or, Les-** sons at Home. A Book for Boys and Girls.

5. **Country Pleasures ; or, The** Carterets. By A. E. R.

6. **Stories of Courage and Prin-** ciple ; or, Fit to be a Duchess. By Mrs. GILLESPIE SMYTH.

7. **Who are the Happy Ones?** or, Home Sketches. By the Author of "Quiet Thoughts for Quiet Hours," &c.

8. **The Progress of Character ;** or, Cliffethorpe. By H. POWER.

9. **What can She Do?** By Rev. E. P. ROE.

Published by Ward, Lock, and Co.

New Books and New Editions.

Beeton's "All About It" Books.

Now Ready, handsomely bound, price 2s. 6d. each.

1. **ALL ABOUT COOKERY**: Being a Dictionary of Every-day Cookery. By Mrs. Isabella Beeton.

2. **ALL ABOUT EVERYTHING**: Being a Dictionary of Practical Recipes and Every-day Information. An entirely New Domestic Cyclopædia, arranged in Alphabetical Order, and usefully Illustrated.

3. **ALL ABOUT GARDENING**: Being a Dictionary of Practical Gardening.

4. **ALL ABOUT COUNTRY LIFE**: A Dictionary of Rural Avocations, and of Knowledge necessary to the Management of the Farm, &c.

5. **ALL ABOUT HARD WORDS**: Being a Dictionary of Every-day Difficulties in Reading, Writing, &c. &c.

Price 1s., cloth, containing 208 pages, 477 Recipes, and Formulæ for Mistresses and Servants. Also, with Coloured Plates, price 1s. 6d.

MRS. BEETON'S ENGLISHWOMAN'S COOKERY BOOK.
Comprising Recipes in all branches of Cookery, and accurate Descriptions of Quantities, Times, Costs, Seasons, for the various Dishes.

. *The capital Coloured Plates render the Eighteenpenny Edition of* The Englishwoman's Cookery Book *absolutely unapproachable in point of excellence and cheapness. There are infinitely more Recipes in this volume than in any other Cheap Cookery Book, their accuracy is beyond question, and the addition of these Coloured Plates removes all possibility of successful rivalry which may be attempted by imitative and meretricious displays.*

Price 3s. 6d., 476 pages, with many Engravings in the Text, and Coloured Plates, exquisitely produced by the best Artists.

BEETON'S EVERY-DAY COOKERY & HOUSEKEEPING BOOK. Comprising Instructions for Mistress and Servants, and a Collection of Practical Recipes. With 104 Coloured Plates, showing the Modern Mode of sending Dishes to Table.

Price 1s., cloth, containing 252 pages; also, with Coloured Plates, price 1s. 6d.

BEETON'S GARDENING BOOK: Containing such full and Practical Information as will enable the Amateur to manage his own Garden. Amply Illustrated.

NEW AND IMPORTANT BOOK OF REFERENCE ON GARDENING.
460 pages, with Coloured Plates and Engravings in the Text, price 3s. 6d.

BEETON'S DICTIONARY OF EVERY-DAY GARDENING: Constituting a Popular Cyclopædia of the Theory and Practice of Horticulture. Embellished with Coloured Plates, made after original Water-colour Drawings copied from Nature.

Published by Ward, Lock, and Co.

𝕭𝖊𝖊𝖙𝖔𝖓'𝖘 𝕷𝖊𝖌𝖆𝖑 𝕳𝖆𝖓𝖉𝖇𝖔𝖔𝖐𝖘.

Now Ready, in strong Linen Covers, price 1s. each.

1. Property.
2. Women, Children, and Registration.
3. Divorce & Matrimonial Causes.
4. Wills, Executors, and Trustees.
5. Transactions in Trade, Securities, and Sureties.
6. Partnership and Joint-Stock Companies.
7. Landlord and Tenant, Lodgers, Rates and Taxes.
8. Masters, Apprentices, Servants, and Working Contracts.
9. Auctions, Valuations, Agency, Games, and Wagers.
10. Compositions, Liquidations, and Bankruptcy.
11. Conveyance, Travellers, and Innkeepers.
12. Powers, Agreements, Deeds, and Arbitrations.

** *These Books are as excellent as they are cheap. The persevering labour devoted to their production has resulted in the classification and completeness which distinguish them among similar attempts. Each one of the series has its own separate Index, and the amount of information is much greater and more varied than the necessary brevity of the title suggests.*

Cloth elegant, gilt edges, price 3s. 6d.

BEETON'S BOOK OF BIRDS; showing How to Rear and Manage them in Sickness and in Health.

** *This volume contains upwards of One Hundred Engravings and Six exquisitely Coloured Plates printed Facsimile from Coloured Sketches by* HARRISON WEIR.

Cloth elegant, gilt edges, price 3s. 6d., uniform with the "Book of Birds."

BEETON'S BOOK of POULTRY & DOMESTIC ANIMALS; showing How to Rear and Manage in Sickness and in Health—Pigeons, Poultry, Ducks, Turkeys, Geese, Rabbits, Dogs, Cats, Squirrels, Fancy Mice, Tortoises, Bees, Silkworms, Ponies, Donkeys, Inhabitants of the Aquarium, &c.

** *This Volume contains upwards of One Hundred Engravings and Five Coloured Plates from Water-Colour Drawings by* HARRISON WEIR.

Price 5s., numerous Illustrations, cloth, gilt edges.

BEETON'S HOUSEHOLD AMUSEMENTS AND ENJOYMENTS. Comprising Acting Charades, Burlesques, Conundrums, Enigmas, Rebuses, and a number of new Puzzles in endless variety. With folding Frontispiece.

In coloured boards, price 6d. (A wonderful Collection of Information.)

BEETON'S COTTAGE MANAGEMENT. Comprising Cookery, Gardening, Cleaning, and Care of Poultry, &c.

Published by Ward, Lock, and Co.

New Books and New Editions.

Half-bound, price 7s. 6d.; half-calf, 10s. 6d.

BEETON'S DICTIONARY OF GEOGRAPHY: A Universal Gazetteer. Illustrated by Coloured Maps, Ancient, Modern, and Biblical. With Several Hundred Engravings of the Capital Cities of the World, English County Towns, the Strong Places of the Earth, and Localities of General Interest, in separate Plates, on Tinted Paper. Containing in all upwards of Twelve Thousand Distinct and Complete Articles. Edited by S. O. BEETON, F.R.G.S.

Now Ready, cloth gilt, 1,536 pages, price 7s. 6d.

BEETON'S LAW BOOK. A Compendium of the Law of England in reference to Property, Family and Commercial Affairs, including References to about Ten Thousand Points of Law, Forms for Legal Documents, with numerous Cases, and valuable ample Explanations. With a full Index—25,000 references, every numbered paragraph in its particular place and under its general head.

How frequently a want is felt of better legal knowledge upon points which continually arise in the practical experience of most persons. To supply this want is the aim of BEETON'S LAW BOOK. It will be found a most valuable and reliable work for consultation on all ordinary legal questions.

Second and Enlarged Edition now Ready, elegantly bound, gilt edges,
Chromic Title and Frontispiece, 7s. 6d.

BEETON'S BOOK OF NEEDLEWORK. Consisting of Instructions, Illustrations, and Designs by English, German, and French Artists. Every Stitch Described and Engraved with the utmost Accuracy, and the Quantity of Material requisite for each Pattern stated. *Comprising* Tatting Patterns, Embroidery Patterns, Crochet Patterns, Knitting and Netting Patterns, Monogram and Initial Patterns, Berlin Wool Instructions, Embroidery Instructions, Crochet Instructions, Knitting and Netting Instructions, Lace Stitches, Point Lace Patterns, Guipure Patterns. In all, upwards of Five Hundred Accurate Patterns, and New and Old Stitches.

*** *Just as* THE BOOK OF HOUSEHOLD MANAGEMENT *takes due precedence of every other Cookery Book, so this extraordinary collection of Needlework Designs will become the book*, par excellence, *for Ladies to consult, both for Instruction in Stitches and all kinds of Work, and Patterns of elegant style and irreproachable good taste.*

Price 7s. 6d., Coloured Plates; half-calf, 10s. 6d.

BEETON'S BOOK OF GARDEN MANAGEMENT. Embracing all kinds of Information connected with Fruit, Flower, and Kitchen Garden Cultivation, Orchid Houses, Bees, &c. &c. Illustrated with Coloured Plates of surpassing beauty, drawn from nature, and numerous Cuts.

Half-bound, price 7s. 6d.; half-calf, 10s. 6d.

BEETON'S BOOK OF HOME PETS: Showing How to Rear and Manage in Sickness and in Health—Birds, Poultry, Pigeons, Rabbits, Guinea Pigs, Dogs, Cats, Squirrels, Tortoises, Fancy Mice, Bees, Silkworms, Ponies, Donkeys, Goats, Inhabitants of the Aquarium, &c. &c. Illustrated by upwards of 200 Engravings and 11 beautifully Coloured Plates by HARRISON WEIR and F. KEYL.

Published by Ward, Lock, and Co.

BROWN'S SATIN POLISH.

Highest Award, Philadelphia, 1876.
Gold Medal, Berlin, 1877.
Highest Award and only Medal,
Paris Exhibition, 1878.
Highest Award, Melbourne, 1881.
Highest Award & only Medal Frankfort A.M., 1881.

Put on by Sponge attached to Wire and Cork in
each bottle.

No Polishing Brush required. Dries in a few minutes.
Can be used by any Lady **without soiling her fingers.**

The "SATIN POLISH" is the most elegant article of the kind ever produced.

LADIES' SHOES, which have become Red and Rough by wearing, are restored to their
original colour and lustre, and will not soil the Skirts when wet.

TARNISHED PATENT LEATHER is improved by it.

For TRAVELLING BAGS, TRUNKS, HARNESS, CARRIAGE TOPS, &c., it is
unequalled. It will not harden the Leather nor crack. It is not a spirit varnish.

Kept by all Wholesale Houses, all first-class Boot and Shoe Stores, and Chemists, in the United Kingdom.

Factories: 133 and 135, Fulton Street, 154 and 156, Commercial Street, BOSTON; 377, St. Paul Street,
MONTREAL; 18 and 20, Norman's Buildings, St. Luke's, LONDON, E.C.

Ingram Content Group UK Ltd.
Milton Keynes UK
UKHW020836190423
420422UK00006B/460

9 780343 498665